The Last Stand

The Last Stand

*Schools, Communities
and the Future of Rural Nova Scotia*

Paul W. Bennett

with

Nova Scotia Small Schools Initiative
Public Interest Research Group

*Kate Oland, Michelle Wamboldt,
Sandra Labor, Randy Delorey,
Leif Helmer, Steven Rhude, and Ron Stockton*

Fernwood Publishing • Halifax & Winnipeg

To small school advocates
— and to all of those committed to revitalizing rural communities

Editing and design: Brenda Conroy
Printed and bound in Canada by Hignell Book Printing

Published in Canada by Fernwood Publishing
32 Oceanvista Lane, Black Point, Nova Scotia, B0J 1B0
and 748 Broadway Avenue, Winnipeg, Manitoba, R3G 0X3
www.fernwoodpublishing.ca

Fernwood Publishing Company Limited gratefully acknowledges the financial support
of the Government of Canada through the Canada Book Fund and the Canada Council
for the Arts, the Nova Scotia Department of Communities, Culture and Heritage,
the Manitoba Department of Culture, Heritage and Tourism under the
Manitoba Publishers Marketing Assistance Program and the Province of Manitoba,
through the Book Publishing Tax Credit, for our publishing program.

Library and Archives Canada Cataloguing in Publication

Bennett, Paul W., 1949-, author

The last stand : communities and the future of rural
Nova Scotia / Paul W. Bennett.

ISBN 978-1-55266-578-7 (pbk.)

1. Education, Rural--Nova Scotia. 2. Rural schools--
Nova Scotia. 3. Nova Scotia--Rural conditions. I. Title.

LC5148.C32N69 2013   306.4309716   C2013-903007-7

Contents

Acknowledgements vii

Introduction: To Save Small Communities, Save the Schools 1
    Rural Schools at the Centre of Sustainable Communities 6

1   The Big Shift: Confronting Demographic
    Gravity and Rural Decline..8

2   The Disturbing Trend: To Foreclosure 18

3   Impact of School Closures: On Communities and Children 24
    Long Bus Rides 26
    The Quality of Education.. 27
    Parent-Community Involvement.................................... 28
    Short-Term Costs.. 29
    Long-Term Costs... 30

4   The Turnaround Strategy: From School Closures
    to Rural Revitalization.. 33
    Suspending the School Closure Process 34
    The Critical Need for a Rural Revitalization Strategy 35

5   Rural Strategy and Curriculum Reform: The Building Blocks 42
    Leadership 47
    Imagining a Larger Vision 47
    Setting Rural Development Priorities................................. 48
    Networked School Communities 49
    Toward a Social Sustainability Framework 50
    Embracing a Rural World View... 52
    Fashioning a Rural, Place-Based Curriculum 53

6   Community-Building: The Case for Public Engagement........... 55
    The Preferred Model — Under the Microscope 57
    Call for a More Democratic and Legitimate Process 60

7   The Response: Mushrooming Popular Support
    and Official Silence 66
    Origins of the Small Schools Initiative................................. 69

8   Pathway to Rural Regeneration: Transforming Small Schools
    into Community Hubs 75
    The Emerging Third Option — Community Hub Schools................. 77
    What Schools Mean to Small Rural Communities 80
    The Rise of the Community Hub Movement.................................... 83

Epilogue: Signs of Hope, Solidarity and Resilience..........................90
    Flashback: The 2011 Weymouth School Uprising.............................90
    The Weymouth March and Rally...92
    Save Small Schools, Revitalize Small Communities...........................94

Appendix A: Schools at the Centre Vision and Recommendations
    (May 15, 2012) 98
    Key Recommendations...98
    Small Schools Delegation 100

Appendix B: Legal Review — The School Review Process 101
    Identification Report..102
    Impact Assessment Report 103
    Study Committee 104
    Public Hearing 104
    Decision 105

Appendix C: "Sunday Drive Hangover": Transportation
    and Rural Community Life 106

Appendix D: Pathway to Rural Regeneration.................................112
    Key Recommendations...112
    Nova Scotia Small Schools Initiative,
    Core Supporters, March 2013 114

Appendix E: News Release — Nova Scotia Education Minister
    Requests Halt to School Closure Process, 3 April, 2013 116

References..118

Index 125

Acknowledgements

Education reform movements tend to be sparked by a few passionate idealists and, every once in a while, they catch fire and exert a measureable impact upon public policy. A prime example of this phenomenon is the Nova Scotia Small Schools Initiative (NSSSI). Out of seeds planted at a Small School Summit in January 2012 came a provincial delegation to the Minister of Education, the widely discussed Schools at the Centre vision and a full-fledged reform movement known as the NSSSI, hailed by the *Chronicle Herald* as the source of an exciting plan for a "new model of schooling" for the twenty-first century.

The Last Stand is, in many ways, a testament to the unbridled passion and iron determination of a band of small school advocates committed to ridding Nova Scotia of a destructive school review for closure process and supplanting it with a community-building process, exemplifying true public engagement and directed toward rural revitalization. As one of the co-founders, I have found it inspiring to meet and engage with an emerging generation of Nova Scotian community leaders. Leif Helmer and Michelle Wambodlt initiated the Small School Summit and put the village of Petite Riviere on the Canadian education reform map. Since the inception of NSSSI, Kate Oland of Middle River, Victoria County, has acted as co-curator of the NSSSI Facebook page and emerged as our resident visionary. Few can match Randy Delorey of Save Community Schools, based in Heatherton, when it comes to providing advice and counsel on the matter of school closures. Lunenburg lawyer Ron Stockton has been a tremendously loyal supporter of the cause, as has Canadian realist painter Steven Rhude of Wolfville. The whole concept of a rural strategy was developed by Sandra Labor, building upon her initial efforts at Shatford Memorial School in Hubbards. Together, they form what we call the Public Interest Research Group, the team that assisted me in preparing our initial May 2012 brief and then contributing to this book.

Much of the material between these covers builds upon the work of the informed education community, including a mixed assortment of academics, journalists, policy wonks and community activists. Our debt to Dr. Michael Corbett of Acadia University's School of Education is clear, just as it is to Dr. David Clandfield, Canada's leading advocate of "community hub schools."

We have also learned a few vitally important lessons about public advocacy from Patricia Elliott and Real Renewal of Regina, Saskatchewan. Nova Scotia's daily newspaper, the *Chronicle Herald*, and its regional bureau reporters, and CBC News Nova Scotia both do a splendid job covering school closures. Special thanks to education reporter Frances Willick of the *Chronicle Herald* for taking the time to look more deeply into provincial education matters. For fresh perspectives and insights into what's really going on in today's schools, I'm indebted to Cathrine Yuill, Peggy Chisholm, Steven Rhude, Anne Totten, Denise Delorey, Larry Donald Haight, Abby Taylor, Alastair Jarvis, Cecil McLeod, Janessa Blauvelt, John Levac, Debbie Francis, Anita MacLellan, Christopher Gill, Barry Olivella, Jens Laursen, Robert N. Berard, Michael Bowen and Matt d'Entremont.

Over the past two years, Saint Mary's University has provided me with an institutional home and the intellectual stimulation of working with undergraduates with an interest in education. Teaching education courses keeps me fresh and provides a regular forum to discuss critical issues in education reform. Thanks to Dean Esther Enns and Dr. Anthony O'Malley for your regular encouragement and support.

Our publisher Errol Sharpe and his team at Fernwood Publishing continue to publish books with a public purpose appealing to critical thinkers and those committed to real change. After collaborating on the earlier book, *Vanishing Schools, Threatened Communities*, it was great to be re-united on this little book project. Special thanks, once again, to the Fernwood team, particularly production coordinator Beverley Rach, copy editor Brenda Conroy, typesetter Deb Mathers, and promotions person Nancy Malek. My final words of heartfelt appreciation go to K. Dianne Bennett, a tremendous source of love and support who, for some inexplicable reason, continues to allow me to roam free, at large, in every corner of Nova Scotia.

To Save Small Communities, Save the Schools

"In rural Canada, schools are more than just places where children and youth earn an education. They are also the hub and lifeblood of the community. When the local school goes, all too often so does the community." — *Beyond Freefall: Halting Rural Poverty*, Final Report of the Standing Senate Committee on Agriculture and Forestry (June 2008)

"I can't imagine a more vexatious problem for government or one with more impact on communities than the disappearing rural school. A community isn't much without a school, yet too many of our small towns and villages are facing life without one.…

It becomes a vicious circle: Enrolment drops, so a school is closed. Once that happens, people won't move to that community, choking off its chances of regaining its vitality or its school." — Dan Leger, *Chronicle Herald*, February 4, 2013

There are really two Nova Scotias. The first is urban and centred around Halifax Regional Municipality (HRM) and Cape Breton Regional Municipality (CBRM), with HRM and the so-called central corridor serving as both the economic engine and place of residence for nearly half the province's population. The other Nova Scotia is primarily rural and small town, covers most of the province's physical space, and remains home to some 45 percent of the population. Great inequalities exist between urban and rural Nova Scotia, with the fault line strongly reflected in the provincial education system, and regionalization of rural education is only contributing to further rural decline. The future of this "other Nova Scotia" is imperiled, sparking this call to action.

Rural and small town Nova Scotia is facing a looming demographic crisis and, without a provincial rural revitalization strategy, will face a bleak future. School closures capture the news headlines, but they signal a more profound trend -- the outward manifestation of a demographic shift of population that threatens to extinguish what remains of Nova Scotia's rural communities.

Such a trend, while powerful and relentless, should not be accepted like the inevitability of gravity. With declining enrollments, education budget cuts are the current reality, but the minister of education and school boards face a bigger challenge — the important need for a new and innovative plan, attuned to the realities of fiscal restraint, that can deliver quality, equitable education in our rural communities. Developing a plan for the future is emerging as the most critical long-term issue facing rural and small town Nova Scotia.

The core of the "Rural Problem" is not the school review process but rather the lack of a well-developed strategy for rural education and sustainability. Formulating such a plan requires time and leadership from the Government of Nova Scotia, spearheaded by the Department of Education, working in concert with other government departments and agencies. It's time to stop the destructive process of school consolidation, which rips the heart out of rural communities. A moratorium on all school closures is an essential step in the process of saving and revitalizing threatened small communities. The review process has become a divisive force, promoting adversarial relationships and undermining confidence in school boards and the entire public school system. With the breathing space the current moratorium now provides, the Government of Nova Scotia should focus its full energies on developing a rural education and sustainability strategy, led by Nova Scotia Education in collaboration Economic and Rural Development and other provincial and municipal agencies.

Schools should be treated as community assets not liabilities. The Nova Scotia Small Schools Initiative (NSSSI) envisions the community school as the potential centre of community-building and development, and thus it should not be abandoned to a school review for closure process. Nova Scotia needs to move schools to the centre of planning for the future. A one-year moratorium and the provincial review of the impact of the school review procedure and regulations should give the province time to explore community-based alternative approaches. The minister and the Department of Education should be charged with developing a community-based model, focusing on finding mutually agreeable solutions that align with rural community development plans. A school review process would then become a last resort, with terms shifting the "burden of proof" to those seeking school shutdowns.

Putting students first must be our priority. This book recommends changes that will benefit thousands of students and their families across Nova Scotia. Our goals are to secure a future for rural education and to sustain smaller communities. In the process we will also have found a way to keep "good schools" with incredibly strong community support from being shuttered and avert the residue of bitterness in the community.

The Nova Scotia Department of Education's 2012 Kids and Learning First plan opens the door a crack to a new way of thinking about educa-

Closed by the South Shore Regional School Board in June 2009, Riverport Consolidated School now stands abandoned and boarded up in the seaside village. During that cycle of closures, it was one of three small schools declared surplus in Lunenburg County, reportedly now costing local taxpayers $75,000 a year to maintain. (Photo: Jens Laursen)

tion. We call upon the minister of education to make good on, and to build upon, that commitment to "protect the quality of education in rural communities." To do so will require a bigger vision, one that embraces what the *Chronicle Herald* calls "a new model of schooling." That vision will grow out of a broader strategy that puts schools at the centre of community-building and rural development.

We can have small schools and a more efficient school system, but it will require new ways of thinking. Suspending the school review process opens the door to a larger project of rural revitalization. Looking to the future, online learning has enormous potential for bridging the geographic distances and enabling us to fashion a community of networked schools. *The Last Stand* is an appeal to the Government of Nova Scotia to step up to the challenge of designing small community schools, modelling sustainable development, and demonstrating that we can deliver education efficiently on a smaller, more human scale.

On May 15, 2012, a Nova Scotia Small Schools Initiative (NSSSI) delegation met with Education Minister Ramona Jennex to present a brief entitled *Schools at the Centre: A Rural Revitalization Strategy for Rural Communities.* Our report tabled the following recommendations:

1. The Minister of Education announce the Department of Education's intention to take the lead in developing a Rural Revitalization Strategy, working in partnership with Economic and Rural Development for an integrated government-wide approach.

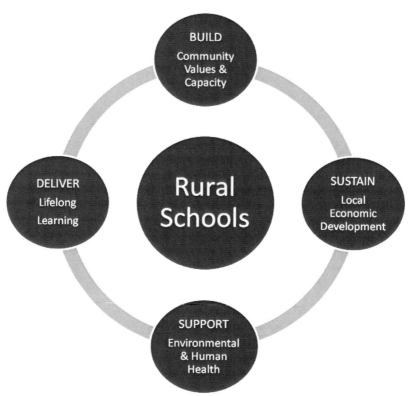

Rural schools should form the centre of sustainable communities. A graphic designed by Sandra Labor for the Small Schools Initiative brief, Schools at the Centre: A Revitalization Strategy for Rural Communities, presented May 15, 2012, to Nova Scotia Education Minister Ramona Jennex.

2. The Minister of Education take the lead in advancing the *Kids & Learning First* plan by embracing our *Schools at the Centre* philosophy aimed at revitalizing rural education through a province-wide, community-building and development strategy.

3. The Minister of Education announce a moratorium on all School Review processes, effective June 1, 2012, affecting all schools recommended for closure in the current provincial cycle of school accommodation reviews.

4. The Department of Education build on the *Nova Scotia Virtual School* project by initiating a Rural Schools Online Education Network, based upon the Newfoundland model, creating digitally-networked schools and taking fuller advantage of distance education in the 21st century guise of virtual schooling.

5. The Department of Education take a lead role in facilitating the partnerships necessary to help small rural communities develop their school structures into multi-use community assets, through a public engagement

process, involving all interested groups, including school boards, regional development agencies, school councils, teachers, local boards of trade, local government and citizens.

After our presentation, the Small Schools Delegation received no official, direct response from the education minister or the Department. The call for a moratorium was quickly rejected in a statement Minister Jennex made to the *Bridgewater Bulletin* and reported in other places. It was clear from the outset that the Department was not prepared for, or equipped to deal with, a report calling for collective action across several government departments. A week after the presentation, the delegation took our case to the Office of the Premier, Darrell Dexter, proposing that it be used as a critical piece in the rural development strategy for the province. We offered to work with the government to advance the strategy of rural revitalization. Again, we received no direct response.

The wheels of change move slowly in Nova Scotia, especially after one issues a clarion call for visionary leadership. Months went by and the Delegation, now known as the Nova Scotia Small Schools Initiative (NSSSI), was left in the dark, awaiting some kind of meaningful reply or any indication that the proposal was being incorporated into future policy initiatives. Then, just as the school review process of 2012–13 came to a head in March 2013 in three of the province's school boards, the Halifax Regional School Board initiated a brand new cycle, putting four more schools up for review. Almost simultaneously, the *Chronicle Herald* ran a three-part series of feature stories entitled "Schools Under Siege," taking dead aim at the contentious and divisive school closure process and touting the Nova Scotia Small Schools Initiative's community hub school model as a viable option for schools and communities under threat (Willick 2013).

What followed was a bombshell announcement. On April 3, 2013, ten months after the NSSSI presentation and with a provincial election in the off-ing, Education Minister Ramona Jennex responded to the mounting public pressure and dropped a policy directive on the province's eight school boards. Days after the so-called "March School Closure Madness" had ended for the season, Jennex called for a suspension of school shutdowns for one year, allowing enough time to develop a new process that was "fairer and better reflects the interests of students and communities" (Nova Scotia Education and Child Development 2013).

What prompted the education minister to act — and what was the NDP government's real end game? A cessation in the school review process signalled what amounted to "a temporary victory" for the Nova Scotia Small Schools Initiative. Yet the official rationale provided by Jennex and the Department made no reference to the NSSSI or its advocacy, and they

Rural Schools at the Centre of Sustainable Communities

"Imagine for a moment a developed nation which regarded its rural schools as its elite and as models to be envied and emulated by metropolitan schools.

Imagine a system in which rural schools were the prime beneficiaries of educational research, the recipients of a steady stream of the nation's best educators, and the bastions of the education world's power, prestige, and resources." — Jonathan P. Sher, General Editor, *Education in Rural America: A Reassessment of Conventional Wisdom* (1978)

"The trend to close schools was intensified by a culturally popular assumption...schools need to be big to be good. In fact, for many decades of the 20th century, school consolidation was considered synonymous with school improvement, despite the fact there was virtually no evidence to support the assumption." — Michael Corbett and Dennis Mulcahy, *Education on a Human Scale: Small Rural Schools in Modern Context* (2006)

"We need a new model of schooling.... a school that can improve services in smaller settings and do it efficiently, too.... What would it look like? It would make more use of expert online courses, with support from onsite teachers — accelerating the plan to triple enrolment and course offerings in the province's Virtual School. There should be less long-distance busing, a waste of time in a digital world. Schools could be in smaller, high-efficiency buildings, or share sites with other services. We can blow money trying to keep inefficient, wrong sized buildings open. Or we can design compact new ones to meet the need to deliver education efficiently on a smaller, local scale." — *Chronicle Herald*, "New Model Schooling," April 17, 2012

appeared to appropriate the community school hub model without acknowledging its origins. Here, in this book, is the behind-the-scenes story of how the Nova Scotia government came to "discover" the plight of rural communities facing school closures. This book demonstrates conclusively that, without a province-wide movement pushing for a fundamental re-thinking of our model of schooling, the trend toward a centralized, bureaucratically driven school system will not be halted, let alone reversed. Indeed, the relentless force of school consolidation and what Halifax pollster Don Mills calls "townsizing" will in all likelihood still spell a death sentence for what's left of rural Nova Scotia.

In the spring of 2013, an engaged public was looking to the Nova Scotia Commission on the New Economy, headed by Acadia University President Ray Ivany, for some creative, innovative policy proposals. The Nova Scotia Small Schools Initiative weighed in on April 2, 2013, with a new brief, entitled *Pathway to Rural Regeneration* (Bennett 2013a). The core message went as follows: Plugging the rural drain should be a higher priority and so should rebuilding social capital in Nova Scotia outside the Halifax Regional Municipality and the central corridor of the province. No small town or village survives very long without schools, young families, and children. We see great potential in transforming small rural schools into vibrant "community hub schools" and are encouraged by community-led hub school initiatives springing-up in pockets of rural Nova Scotia. It's also time to look at developing a more explicit rural, place-based curriculum better attuned to the interests and needs of the children (Corbett 2006). Building upon these local school initiatives will ultimately prove to be the surest route to rural regeneration in Nova Scotia and far beyond in the years ahead.

This book is a *cri de coeur* for rural and small town Nova Scotia. It also is the story of the rise of the Nova Scotia small schools movement from the ringing of the initial alarm bells in the spring of 2011 to the education minister's April 2013 suspension of the Nova Scotia school review process. In recounting the story, we hope to inspire Nova Scotians to take up the cause and join in the struggle to save our vanishing small schools and threatened rural communities.

1

The Big Shift
Confronting Demographic Gravity and Rural Decline

"All growth in Nova Scotia is being concentrated around what's called the growth corridor, (which is) basically around HRM.... We're getting this rural-urban divide that's going to become a more serious problem in the future, not less serious." — Mike Foster, President of Canmac Economics Limited, presenting *Nova Scotia Regions Demographic Outlook*, Union of Nova Scotia Municipalities, November 2012

"Traditional economic growth models and approaches provide and suggest a gloomy picture and future for rural Nova Scotia communities. A broader perspective that recognizes the vitality and creativity of persons choosing to live in rural Nova Scotia must be pursued. The reality, however, is such that help is needed to develop and sustain the rural way of life that encompasses social, cultural, economic, and environmental objectives." — Dennis Pilkey, *Rural Development Assessment*, Final Report for Coastal Communities Network, March 2009, p. 41

Since June of 2012, Don Mills, Chief Executive Officer of Corporate Research Associates, has issued a series of warnings that Nova Scotia's economy was in deep trouble. If Nova Scotia is to improve its economic outlook, he told the Pictou County Chamber of Commerce in Stellarton, people must be open to change, particularly with regard to improving marketing through amalgamating municipal governance units (Gorman 2012). Mills claimed that the lack of private sector growth throughout the province was a real source of concern and something that will keep the province in the "have-not" status until it is addressed. Interviewed on *CBC News* on February 5, 2013, the Halifax pollster went much further: "We're not that attractive a place to live in terms of the economy we have in this region.... At least 45 percent of the population lives in communities of fewer than 5,000 people, but only 20 percent of the rest of Canada is considered rural.... We have

One of many Nova Scotia rural schools declared "surplus" and now surviving as a re-purposed community centre in Queen's County on the South Shore. After closure, local municipalities scramble to find new tenants in communities emptying of young families. (Personal Collection)

failed to urbanize and this is holding us back." Moving to larger centres is called "townsizing," he pointed out, and increased townsizing would be better for the future of rural Nova Scotians.

Don Mills' dire warnings raised the ire of rural Nova Scotians and set the heather on fire. The NDP government of Darrell Dexter was shaken by his interventions because they occurred just as the Nova Scotia Commission on Building Our New Economy, headed by Acadia University President Ray Ivany, was preparing to launch its initial round of public consultations. The provincial commission, branding itself *OneNovaScotia.ca* and seeking to restore public confidence, would not be aided by such divisive pronouncements. One of the commission's five members, John Bragg, President and CEO of Oxford Frozen Foods, the world's blueberry products king, was not amused. His home town of Oxford, on the North Shore, had a population of far fewer than 5,000, insufficient to be a candidate for townsizing. Bringing the urban-rural divide into sharper relief was not part of the building a One Nova Scotia plan.

The Ivany Commission, announced on November 29, 2012, aroused new hopes in rural and small town Nova Scotia. Premier Dexter presented the commission as a way of promoting and spreading out economic growth, leveraging the Irving Shipyard Contract, boosting offshore exploration, spurring innovations in the forestry sector, and capitalizing on the Maritime Link power line between Cape Breton and Newfoundland. "I want Nova Scotians to understand that growth in one part of the province means opportunity in the others," Dexter declared. "I want to break down the outdated idea that regions of the province are competing against each other." Chair Ivany followed suit, emphasizing the goal of "maximizing the shipbuilding contract," which could "add up to as much as $25 billion" and its potential for spinoffs like "new technologies" (Jackson 2012).

While Premier Dexter saw the commission as advancing his "Jobs Start Here" agenda, influential voices saw in the venture a real opportunity to tackle rural decline and uneven development. The Oxford Foods magnate John Bragg, described by Toronto business reporter Gordon Pitts as a cross between a country squire and a tough, risk-taking tycoon, saw the commission's mandate through a different lens: "I think the metro area is in a pretty healthy situation, but I think we could all agree that rural areas need some attention of some kind" (Pitts 2012). Living on the North Shore, he was acutely aware of the formidable challenge facing threatened rural communities. "If we're not careful, the infrastructure will disappear, the schools will disappear, and nobody will live in these towns, and then we'll wake up 20 to 30 years from now and say 'Why did we allow this to happen?'" (Jackson 2012).

Appointing the commission raised expectations that the plight of rural Nova Scotia was finally on the provincial policy radar. In addition to the clumsy handling of the Yarmouth ferry and the elimination of protected Acadian electoral districts, the Dexter government was mired in disputes with rural communities over salmon acquaculture, mink farms, and wind turbines. Amidst that spreading thicket of rural concerns, the creation of the economic commission and a re-organization of Nova Scotia's Regional Development Authorities (RDAs) seemed to signal a new commitment to rebuilding the damaged relations with rural communities. An editorial in the province's newspaper of record, the *Chronicle Herald*, on November 30, 2012, described the two initiatives as moves that "hit the reset button on rural Nova Scotia." Whatever the motive, the editorial said, "serious consultation on how to boost growth outside Halifax is in order." The commission was welcomed for its "sensible mandate" to "treat the province as an integrated whole" and take advantage of "every opportunity" right across the province. Reforming the RDA system (renamed Regional Enterprise Networks) by cutting the number from twelve to six agencies was hailed as a healthy step, paving the way for the streamlining, partnering, and integrating of business development strategies and services. Taken together, the initiatives were praised for setting the stage for "real progress toward maximizing growth opportunities in the province."

The commission led off with what Ray Ivany termed "a bucket of ice water," then promoted a positive, upbeat message during its province-wide winter and spring 2013 consultations. The opening presentation looked at the province's economic and demographic plight, highlighting the sluggish growth, population losses, low productivity, and out-migration of workers. Most of the sessions held in World Café style discussion groups were designed to generate ideas, promote common understanding, and stimulate innovation. The guided discussions reflected the narrow "economic lens" adopted by the commission. Instead of focusing on the urban-rural divide, the commission adopted the mantra of "wealth creation" and "spreading out prosperity" across the province (Jeffrey 2013). In the words of its Information Sheet, "The Commission is focusing on the need to create new wealth in Nova Scotia. To live the lives we want to live, to be communities where people of all ages and origins choose to live, work, and play, and to have quality services and amenities accessible to all, we need the ongoing creation of wealth" (Nova Scotia Commission on the New Economy 2013: 1).

In spite of its good intentions, the Ivany Commission was swimming upstream and appeared to be gliding over the deep divisions and inequalities readily apparent across the province. The economic and demographic outlook was decidedly grim, and much of that was starkly revealed in the population drain from rural to urban centres and from Nova Scotia to Alberta and other points west. With a 2011 population of 945,457, up 0.1 percent from the previous year, Nova Scotia was stagnating and facing the prospect of serious demographic decline between now and 2026. An aging population, inter-provincial out-migration, and modest international immigration spelled trouble, but the internal movement of people to the "middle of Nova Scotia" — Halifax and the central corridor — was even more worrisome. The biggest surprise provided by the NDP government-appointed commission was the scant attention paid to the urban-rural divide and the implicit acceptance of market forces in determining the shape of rural development.

The initial approach of the Ivany commission was remarkably consistent with the business development model promoted by Deloitte management's *The Future of Productivity* initiative as part of its "eight-step game plan for Canada." The clear priority was addressing the Atlantic region's productivity challenge and, specifically, Nova Scotia's "lag in labour productivity" (Deloitte 2012: 4–30). It also echoed the position expressed in a May 24, 2012, presentation sponsored by the Greater Halifax Partnership, chief proponent of the "Halifax Hub" strategy for driving provincial economic development (2). In many ways, the commission was simply a further manifestation of the NDP government's "Jobs Start Here" promotional campaign. Even NDP sympathizers, like veteran journalist Ralph Surette of Yarmouth, expressed public concern over Premier Dexter's "jobs obsession" and delay in getting "new rural development initiatives" underway (Surette 2012).

The long cycle of rural economic and demographic decline was not only well documented, but it had been indentified as a priority for provincial action by the Union of Nova Scotia Municipalities (UNSM) and rural development groups, including the Coastal Communities Network. In October 2012, Mike Foster, President of Canmac Economics, told a UNSM conference that the rural decline in Nova Scotia was deepening. Based upon an analysis of 2011 Canada Census data, he reported that HRM was experiencing "fairly strong urbanization" and had grown by 4.6 percent from 2006 to 2011. Although Antigonish and the odd other town had grown slightly, the vast majority of villages and towns registered "negative growth rates" over that five-year period. "All growth in Nova Scotia is being concentrated around what's called the growth corridor, essentially around HRM," Foster stated. Fourteen years from now, he forecast, unless policies change, regions like Cape Breton, the Annapolis Valley, and the South Shore will experience significant population decreases. The bottom line, for Foster, was crystal clear: "We're getting this urban-rural divide and that's going to become a more serious problem in the future, not less serious" (Lightstone 2012).

The Canmac Economics *Demographic Outlook* report on Nova Scotia regions was alarming and hard to ignore, especially outside of HRM. The report forecast that Nova Scotia's population would grow, albeit slowly, from 921,720 in 2011 to reach 932,967 in 2021, and then fall to 926,565 by 2026. With the province's aging population and inter-provincial losses, the only real increases would come as a result of international immigration. Most significant of all, for the Nova Scotia school system, the bottom was going to fall

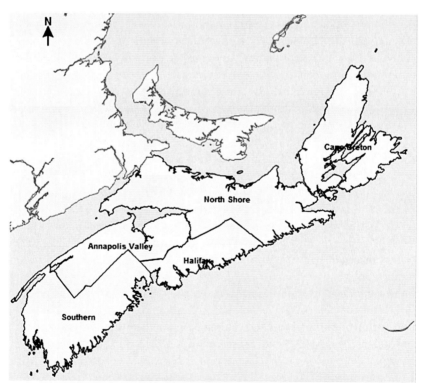

A 2012 Canmac Economics Demographic Outlook report to the Union of Nova Scotia Municipalities divided the province into five distinct regions for economic and social development forecasts.

Table 1.1 Regional Population Trends, 1996 to 2011s

Region	1991	1996	2001	2006	2011
Annapolis Region	117,801	121,000	121,152	122,655	123,649
Cape Breton Region	161,686	158,271	147,454	142,298	135,974
Halifax Region	330,846	342,966	359,183	372,858	390,328
North Shore Region	162,568	162,255	158,282	156,476	155,969
Southern Region	127,041	124,790	121,936	119,175	116,080
Total	899,942	909,282	908,007	913,462	921,727

Source: Statistics Canada, Census of Canada

Table 1.2 Nova Scotia Regional Populations % Change

Region	1996	2001	2006	2011
Annapolis Region	2.72	0.13	1.24	0.81
Cape Breton Region	-2.11	-6.83	-3.50	-4.44
Halifax Region	3.66	4.73	3.81	4.69
North Shore Region	-0.19	-2.45	-1.14	-0.50
Southern Region	-1.77	-2.29	-2.26	-2.60

Source: Statistics Canada, Census of Canada, calculated by Canmac Economics.
Note: The demographic outlook is gloomy in the absence of a rural strategy aimed at ensuring economic and social sustainability. The Halifax Region was the only region that has experienced growth (+4.69%) from 1996 until 2011 and both Caspe Breton (-4.44) and the Southern Region (-2.60) suffered net losses in population.

out of student enrolment. Between 2011 and 2026, the age five to nineteen population is forecast to decline from 151,680 to 127,419, or by some 24,261 children, amounting to a significant drop of 15.9 percent. If demographic trends remain unaltered, three of the province's five regions will suffer net losses in numbers of residents. While HRM will grow in overall population by 4.9 percent over the next fifteen years, Cape Breton, the South Shore and the Northern Region will all lose population (Canmac 2012a: 3, 8–9).

A snapshot of Nova Scotia in 2006, prepared by Dartmouth consultant Dennis Pilkey for the Coastal Communities Network in 2009, bore down more deeply into the economic and demographic plight of rural areas and the poorer coastal communities. In his 2009 *Rural Development Assessment* report, Pilkey points out that Nova Scotia is "uniquely positioned in Canada" because of its higher rural population, averaging between 60 and 75 percent of the total, depending upon the classification criteria. In 2006, some 54 percent of the population lived in places of less than 5,000 inhabitants. If Cape Breton is counted as rural, then the figure rose to 63 percent of the population. From a different vantage point, some 53 percent of the popula-

Table 1.3 Population Forecast: School Age Population and Aging of the Population, 2011-2026

Age	2011	2016	2021	2026
0–4 years	43,980	43,821	43,080	40,524
5 to 9 years	44,425	42,108	41,962	41,277
10 to 14 years	49,815	45,041	42,752	42,608
15 to 19 years	57,440	50,485	45,786	43,534
20 to 24 years	59,615	55,868	48,948	44,267
25 to 29 years	51,925	55,089	51,345	44,428
30 to 34 years	51,540	53,114	56,358	52,519
35 to 39 years	56,385	52,069	53,592	56,744
40 to 44 years	62,110	57,649	53,405	54,901
45 to 49 years	76,280	63,511	59,106	54,919
50 to 54 years	77,460	77,494	65,010	60,704
55 to 59 years	70,955	77,970	77,995	65,867
60 to 64 years	66,430	71,159	77,914	77,920
65 to 69 years	48,920	63,650	68,071	74,319
70 to 74 years	36,400	46,175	59,705	63,835
75 to 79 years	27,655	31,342	39,567	50,910
80 to 84 years	20,015	21,864	24,732	31,080
85 to 89 years	12,735	13,387	14,527	16,431
90+	7,635	8,527	9,111	9,780
Total	921,720	930,324	932,967	926,565

Source: Econometric Folder/subregion model/Nova Scotia Demographic Forecast Model (2007–2031) copy.

Note: The school and college age population (5 to 19 and 20 to 24 years) is expected to suffer significant losses from 2011 to 2026. Some 151,680 children ages 5 to 19 were recorded in 2011, but the numbers drop by 16 per cent (24,311) over the next 15 years. The college and university age population eligible cohort (ages 20 to 24) is forecasted to decline from 59,615 to 44,267, a staggering 25.7 per cent. (Canmac Economics).

tion lived in coastal communities, including a surprising 16 percent inside the Halifax Regional Municipality.

School-age population declines are far from a new phenomenon. The Canmac forecast to 2026 is consistent with the trend in recent decades. The Coastal Communities Network study shows that, between 1991 and 2006, the numbers of children aged under twenty plummeted by 17 percent, led by Metro Cape Breton (-33 percent) and rural coastal areas (- 27 percent).

In rural, inland communities, Pilkey found that the decline was 16 percent, 6 percent higher than the 10 percent loss registered by HRM coastal communities. A more detailed analysis of household income by community, utilizing 2006 Nova Scotia Community Counts data, provides rare insight into the growing economic inequalities between urban and rural communities. From 1996 to 2006, the poorest communities, measured by household income, were getting poorer, and most of them were First Nations communities with median incomes ranging from 34 percent (Eskasoni) to 67 percent (Millbrook) of the Nova Scotia average. Within HRM, thirty-one of the forty-three communities registered median household incomes above the provincial average. Rural communities, with a few isolated exceptions, had lower average and median incomes. No local communities in Annapolis County had median incomes more than 85 percent of the provincial average, communities in Guysborough County ranged from 67–87 percent of the average, and communities in Cumberland County ranged from 70–92 percent of the average. On the Nova Scotia South Shore, median household incomes also lagged behind in Shelburne and Queens counties. In Pictou County, median income levels varied widely, from 86 percent in River John to 115 percent in Scotsburn and 147 percent in Little Harbour. Up in Cape Breton, outside of CBRM, Inverness, and Baddeck, all communities had below average median household incomes (Pilkey 2009: 54–65). In short, the 2006 Community Counts data made visible stark inequalities between urban and rural communities.

The Coastal Communities Network report contends that "traditional economic growth models and approaches provide and suggest a gloomy picture and future for rural Nova Scotia communities." It recommends taking a different tack. "A broader perspective that recognizes the vitality and creativity of persons choosing to live in rural Nova Scotia must be pursued. The reality, however, is such that help is needed to develop and sustain the rural way of life that encompasses social, cultural, economic, and environmental objectives" (Pilkey 2009: 41). Simply put, rural development needs are unique and require a far more comprehensive strategy than traditional business promotion models focusing on resource industries, call centres, and similar "job creation" ventures.

Demographic shifts are going to further accentuate the urban-rural divide. A December 2006 report conducted by Dr. Jim McNiven for Canmac Economics made a clear distinction between the areas surrounding HRM and the rest of the province. Based upon an analysis of the 1996 to 2005 period, counties within a ninety-minute commute to downtown Halifax experienced stable or slight population growth. Eleven counties, the study found, suffered declines, from 1.7 percent in Yarmouth to 17.2 percent in Guysborough County. By 2026, according to this forecast, HRM will accommodate nearly half the Nova Scotia population, and when the four closest counties (Lunenburg, Kings, Hants, and Colchester) are included, that proportion reaches 70 percent (McNiven 2006: 3, 13). Without any change in strategic direction, rural and small town Nova Scotia will be left behind and consigned to a lesser existence.

The public release of the 2011 Canadian Census results for Nova Scotia was another shocker for both politicians and rural Nova Scotians. A front-page story in the *Chronicle Herald* on February 9, 2012, screamed: "Parties play census blame game." It was precipitated by a Statistics Canada report identifying Nova Scotia as "the country's laggard in population growth." Between 2006 and 2011, the province's population grew by only 0.9 percent, or 8,265 people, the lowest among the provinces and half that of the next lowest, Newfoundland and Labrador. The report confirmed that, within Nova Scotia, while Halifax grew by 4.7 percent, twelve of eighteen counties, mostly rural, registered declines. Minister of Economic and Rural Development Percy Paris was caught off guard but responded by deflecting the responsibility, noting that the slide began long before the NDP assumed power in 2009. Mega projects were to be the province's economic salvation. When pressed, Paris claimed that the province was on the cusp of a reversal. Major projects like the $25 billion shipbuilding project, the Lower Churchill hydroelectric project, and Shell Oil's six-year, off-shore exploration plan were trotted out to make the case that the province was on the verge of an economic recovery. It was left to Cape Breton political scientist David Johnson to cut to the heart of the matter. Drastic population declines were going to pose challenges in sustaining public services in the rural mainland and Cape Breton. "You will see that in public schools … whether schools should be closed in those areas.… We see the same type of debate over hospitals.… You see the same pressure on public libraries" (Jackson 2012a). All of this was assuming, of course, that the only real option was consolidation of services in rural and small town Nova Scotia.

Something unexpected happened in response to the body blow administered by the 2011 Census and its bleak economic and demographic findings. Instead of accepting the dictates of demographic gravity, small rural communities threatened with school and hospital closures began fighting back. The *Chronicle Herald*, guided by Associate Publisher Ian Thompson and Editor Bob Howes, came out strongly in favour of developing a "new model of schooling" reflecting the changing demographics and latest advances in learning technologies. When it was learned that the Nova Scotia public school system had 5 million square feet of excess classroom space, the paper went on record recommending that the Education Department and the school boards move "aggressively to sell-off surplus and unsuitable schools" and, instead of erecting massive schools, spend the proceeds building "modern, smaller, better-equipped, and cheaper-to-run schools that actually fit the needs of the student populations and the communities of today and tomorrow."

The editorial, entitled "Old Schools for New," published on November 28, 2012, categorically rejected "more school consolidation and long-distance bus rides," claiming "We've probably taken that model as far as it should go. We think the province should invest in a new model of school that can deliver quality education in a smaller community setting — the education equivalent of what Community Emergency Centres are doing in health care. Sometimes it will also make sense for these smaller community schools to share a building with other community services."

The paradigm shift exemplified in the editorial cannot come fast enough for hard pressed and neglected rural communities. Those living in more remote rural areas of Nova Scotia have a right to feel that their interests are not being fully addressed by any level of government, including the school boards. That view, held by many rural Nova Scotians, was strongly voiced in Maurice Rees's March 2013 *Shoreline Journal* column, "Are you feeling marginalized?" Rees raised a whole raft of concerns ranging from the wasting of taxpayers' money to poor Internet services to pot-hole filled roads. "The loss of schools, gas stations, and shopping," he wrote, " causes rural residents to spend their hard earned dollars in areas other than where they live." It was all part of a vicious cycle, according to Rees: "Declining population and an aging population results in less school age students, hence school boards find reasons to close (mostly elementary) schools adding to the demise of rural areas. A way must be found to reduce the frequency of school closures. There are things that can be done to stop the off-loading of Department of Education expenses to another jurisdiction."

2

The Disturbing Trend
To Foreclosure

"At the precise time that the more affluent provinces… are introducing education choice and smaller, more specialized schools, Nova Scotia is planning for consolidation and standardization — the ultimate 'one-size-fits all' education with a few untidy outliers." — Paul W. Bennett, *Vanishing Schools, Threatened Communities* (2011), p. 180

"Smaller schools, like smaller towns, generate higher expectations for mutual reciprocity and collective action. So deconcentrating megaschools or creating smaller 'schools within schools' will almost certainly produce civic dividends." — Robert Putnam, *Bowling Alone: The Collapse and Revival of American Community* (2001), p. 405

Declining student enrolments and school closures were by the early 2000s a well established fact of life throughout rural and small town Nova Scotia. School consolidation, coming in successive waves, was widely viewed with the suspicion reserved for relentless and threatening social forces (Bennett 2011: 149–50). The school review process had also emerged as a lightning rod in many rural communities with schools listed for possible closure. By 2005–06, public opposition to the process mounted, eventually prompting a provincial response.

Challenges to the legitimacy of the existing "consultation process" and stiff resistance from local municipalities, particularly in Chignecto-Central and Cape Breton-Victoria regions, caught the attention of Dr. John Hamm of Pictou County and his Conservative government. His education minister, Jamie Muir, announced in March 2006 a comprehensive review of legislation covering the school closure process and a moratorium on school closures, pending completion of the review. "Reviewing schools for possible permanent closure is a challenging task, fraught with emotion and fear of the unknown," Muir stated. While school closures would continue to be necessary, he said that the government wanted to be sure that "the mandated process" was "the right process" for students, the system, and local communities. Behind the scenes, Muir and the Department were concerned over the ferocity of local

A show of village solidarity in front of Rev. H.J. MacDonald School (P–6) in Heatherton, Antigonish County. After a four-year-long school closure battle, the school closed in June 2012 and a group of parents lost a court challenge in the Delorey v SRSB (2013) decision. (Photo: Randy Delorey)

opposition and the province's capacity to withstand legal challenges based upon claims that the boards acting precipitously had violated the accepted rules for due process (NSDoE 2006).

One of the major inhibiting factors was the simple logistical problem presented by consolidations that put more students on buses travelling longer and longer distances. In the United States, long school bus rides were becoming a major political issue, especially rural West Virginia and small town Ohio. Beginning in 1999, local taxpayers revolted against the mounting bus transportation levies. A well-organized West Virginia small schools coalition of parents charged that long bus rides were prolonging the school day and "stealing the joy of childhood." Rural education researchers in Ohio produced a damning report in the fall of 2005 confirming the existence of widespread parent resistance to long bus rides (Bennett 2011: 155).

In the case of Nova Scotia, the moratorium on school closures announced by Education Minister Muir in March 2006 ended up lasting over two full years. In the interim, school boards continued to compile their lists of schools for possible closure. During the hiatus, the fate of many Nova Scotia schools hung in the balance, including four in Chignecto-Central Region: River Hebert High, Wentworth Elementary, Trenton Elementary, and Thorburn Consolidated. When a new minister, Karen Casey, lifted the moratorium, the real intent of the pause became abundantly clear. The suspension of the freeze was coupled with the implementation of a new school review process. After a detailed review, including a test of legality, the Department acted upon seven recommendations aimed at "making school reviews more open and transparent." Reacting to the voices of critics and the threat of potentially costly legal challenges, Minister Casey insisted that the legislation established "a very public and thorough process that school boards must follow" (*Amherst Daily News*, April 9, 2008).

School boards were now expected to do their homework in preparing for school closures. The facilities-planning formula based upon balancing student numbers was no longer good enough to guarantee success. School boards now had to produce "impact assessment reports" explaining why a school was being considered for closure. That report, modelled after those in Ontario and fine-tuned by former Superintendent James Gunn, was to provide a coherent rationale, encompassing historical and projected enrolment data, local demographic trends, and an assessment of the building's physical condition. Curiously absent from the stated assessment criteria was any attempt to correlate school size with the quality of education. Lifting the moratorium only signalled a resumption of the ongoing march of further consolidation under new rules of engagement (Bennett 2011: 160).

School consolidation continued to be central to Nova Scotia Education's future planning. In March 2007, Gunn produced a revealing research report for the Department. In his new guise as a government consultant, Gunn analyzed the grim enrolment forecasts and offered some pragmatic system-wide restructuring proposals. Nova Scotia's school enrolment was dropping with what seemed like the force of a lead weight. Whereas total enrolment had dipped by 13 percent from 1995 to 2005, it was forecast to drop by 24 percent to only 114,600 students over the next ten years (Gunn 2007a).

Gunn pointed to a major shift with serious implications. While high school enrolment had only declined by 5 percent over the previous decade, it would drop by 21 percent over the next one. Likewise and just as extreme, the junior high enrolment decline would jump from 8 percent to 25 percent. Totalling the shortfalls, he estimated that Nova Scotia was going to have 17,000 fewer junior and senior high school students by 2015–16. Assuming an average school size of 450 students, the report forecast that Nova Scotia would need thirty-eight fewer secondary schools.

If a Nova Scotia enrolment "crisis" lay ahead, the Department would take it in stride. Declining enrolments were hardly new, and somehow the system found a way to adapt and carry on without too many ripples. Yet Gunn's report was different; it was a shocking wake-up call. His conclusion was uncharacteristically blunt: "The potential impact on the delivery of programs on secondary schools and on the efficient use of existing school facilities needs immediate attention." Muddling through was no longer an option. Without changing the grade configurations and juggling students and teachers, over thirty high schools were going to be surplus to the system (Bennett 2011: 150).

After analyzing enrolment trends and "grade level configuration" research, Gunn saw no alternative but further consolidation: "With an increasing abundance of unused classrooms at the junior and senior high levels, these schools could be reconfigured to take in more grade levels." Current high schools serving Grades 10 to 11, Gunn suggested, "could become 9–12 schools or even 7–12 schools, with Grade 9 accommodated as a transitional year." He also recommended "super sizing" for the province's elementary schools. At the lower levels, that could very well mean converting some elementary schools to P–8 schools, or converting middle/junior highs into P–8 schools. Gazing into the future, Dr. Gunn envisioned that "expanding the grade configurations" would return to use the increasing number of "unused classrooms" across Nova Scotia. The proposed restructuring, based upon P–8 and 9–12 grade configurations, was presented as the soundest, most viable option. It could be done, he assured his Education Department colleagues, in standard edu-babble phrasing, "without compromising the educational benefits for students" (Gunn 2007a: 19–20).

Gunn's initial report was followed with a position paper entitled *Optimal School Size* in October 2007. Building upon his initial study, he proceeded to assess research on school size and educational effectiveness. He focused almost exclusively on four American studies tending to favour small schools over large ones and identifying optimal size limits. While Gunn did reference Michael Corbett and Dennis Mulcahy's *Education on a Human Scale*, he was surprisingly dismissive, even though it was the only Canadian study available on the subject. In his view, Corbett and Mulcahy focused on supporting small schools and their study was off-topic. Their study was, Gunn wrote rather tersely, "not about optimal school size in the context of economy of scale and efficient use of school facilities as a scarce resource of a province." Side-stepping the whole issue of educational quality, Gunn simply found that it "casts no light on the numerical measures which define and distinguish small and large" (2007b: 1, 5, 6–8). Simply put, Nova Scotia Education could safely ignore its findings.

The new school review process, established in April 2008, was clearer and more explicit in its requirements. School boards readily embraced the new regulations and saw them as a way of driving "school improvement" as well as fending off legal challenges. School closures resumed as soon as the moratorium was lifted, albeit under

Jens Laursen, veteran of the School Reform struggle, in front of the abandoned Riverport District Consolidated School in March 2013.

A group of Maitland Elementary School kids frolic in front of the Public Hearing Sign at the school in February 2013.

a new set of rules. Well-publicized school closure battles in the Antigonish County (Strait RSB), Colchester County (Chignecto-Central RSB), Riverport (South Shore RSB), and South End Halifax (Halifax RSB), sparked "Save our School" groups and led to calls for another review of the whole process.

The School Review Process Focus Group was initiated in March 2009 to improve the regulations, as a direct result of concerns raised by Jens Laursen and Lori Keelty of Lunenburg County. Six School Advisory Council/community participants found themselves engaged in a focus group where they were a distinct minority, specifically a quarter of the twenty-one representatives. The focus group was mandated to improve the school review process and especially to provide support for School Study Committees. It proposed nine changes to the regulations.

The focus group process proved to be largely fruitless. School boards gained more time to prepare their impact assessment reports (from 61 to 162 days), the School Study Committees lost preparation time (from 147 to 98 days), and a compromise measure guaranteeing "a knowledgeable, third party facilitator/consultant" fell through in the end. After unproductive communications with senior Department of Education officials, all six SAC/community participants signed a dissenting letter on July 6, 2009, to the minister expressing displeasure with the outcome. This again fell on deaf ears (NSSSI 2012).

Parent groups in Nova Scotia became aware of the research funded by the Bill and Melinda Gates Foundation in support of small schools. Memorial University professor Dennis Mulcahy and other small school movement leaders documented the detrimental effects of longer bus rides on children and began pressing governments to look for alternatives. In October 2009, Mulcahy claimed that school boards were testing the limits of student endurance. As long as rural communities continued to exist, he claimed, education authorities should find other ways to serve those communities, exploring a variety of options from smaller school sizes to multi-grade classes to web-based distance education (Mulcahy 2009).

The school review process, as reintroduced in September 2009, was simply not finding community-based solutions. It continued to be based upon a legalistic, adversarial model which pits the school boards against their own communities. Most of the "school hearings" were win-lose confrontations that left lasting wounds. The Education Act still put the onus on the School Study Committee of parent volunteers to secure a reprieve from an impending closure. The school review process not only reaped deep social divisions but undermined support for public education in rural communities like Riverport, Heatherton, Weymouth, Middle River, Bass River, and Newport Station (NSSSI 2012). That, perhaps more than anything else, prompted Education Minister Ramona Jennex's surprise intervention on April 3, 2013, requesting all school boards to suspend closures for a year.

3

Impact of School Closures
On Communities and Children

"In the emerging twenty-first century education order, the student's journey will commence earlier and extend even longer. It will begin with full day primary for four-year olds and pass through enlarged elementary schools to city and regional high schools resembling airport terminals or suburban 'big box' stores. In rural areas, students will be confined to super-sized regional education centres for their entire P-12 education. The highest stage of the bureaucratic education state will be upon us." — Paul W. Bennett, *Vanishing Schools, Threatened Communities* (2011), pp. 180–81

The school review process has been an endurance test for rural schools, students, and families. Leading small school advocates such as Kate Oland of Middle River, Victoria County, Randy Delorey of Heatherton, Antigonish County, and Michelle Wamboldt of Petite Riviere on the South Shore, all veterans of recent struggles, testify to the devastating effect of the school review process on children, families, schools, and communities. Despite the re-tooling of the school review legislation that took place in 2008, the process continues to exert extreme pressure on rural public school supporters, leaving them feeling exhausted, disempowered, and alienated from the system (Oland 2012).

Although the Nova Scotia Small Isolated Schools Supplement (which replaced the Small Schools Grant in 2012) ostensibly protects rural schools, the reality is that many of the funded schools are placed under review year after year, and therefore exist under a cloud of uncertainty. Some parents choose to send their children to the proposed "receiving school" in order to avoid disruption in their schooling. This type of transfer (typically permitted by boards despite policies which generally call for valid educational reasons for transfers), contributes to the community schools' population decline and often creates serious rifts within communities.

For School Study Committees, the task of fighting to save their school is onerous. Communities often struggle to find people with skills appropriate to the task of parsing and responding to the notoriously inaccurate and inadequately referenced impact assessment reports. Despite the oft-repeated assertion that "school review is not about closing schools," the process is uniformly described by participants as being adversarial. Nobody ever feels that their school is being reviewed in order to improve services or provide additional supports.

Committees volunteer the equivalent of thousands of dollars worth of time — time taken away from their children, families, work, and other volunteer commitments. They may incur out-of-pocket costs or experience financial impacts due to lost work opportunities. They also take on the emotional burden of defending their school on behalf of the community. The strain on family life, the extreme time commitment, and the drain on community resources affects everyone (Oland 2012).

School communities feel the strain as well. Small, rural schools often operate like extended families, with teachers who are deeply invested in their students and proud of their school's "culture." Community members often play integral roles within the school, and children feel safe and surrounded by caring adults they know and trust. School reviews threaten that sense of safety. It is akin, on some levels, to a child being told that her family may be breaking up.

School reviews send the message that the community is under attack and under-valued by "the system." In rural areas struggling to retain vital

Students at Rev. H.J. MacDonald School in Heatherton board the bus for the return trip home in rural East Antigonish, April 2010. With school rural consolidation, many rural students now spend over two hours a day riding school buses. (Private collection)

services, the psychological impact cannot be over emphasized. Citizens lose faith in the school board and in the education system (Oland 2012).

Long Bus Rides

"Schools should not be closed if they are a considerable distance from the next school; putting students, especially in elementary school years, on long bus rides is undesirable." — Ben Levin, *Steps to Effective and Sustainable Public Education in Nova Scotia* (2011)

"Too often, in the absence of systematic research, school leaders consider only the practicalities of bus rides rather than considering the effects of bus rides on students' school performance and home lives." — Rob Ramage and Aimee Howley, "Parents' Perceptions of the Rural School Bus Ride," *Rural Educator* (2005)

When rural schools close, children often pay the price in long, unsupervised bus rides. Although current Canadian research is sparse, existing research and anecdotal evidence is clear: Long bus rides affect children's health, erode family and play time, decrease physical activity, diminish participation in extracurricular activities, and may affect educational performance (Fox 1996). The body of research found within the *Guidelines for Child and Youth-Friendly Land-use and Transport Planning in Rural Areas* (O'Brien and Gilbert 2010) clearly demonstrates the toll that transporting children takes on their health and overall well-being. Rural youth are considered to have a greater risk related to obesity and lack of physical activity and are more susceptible to health problems related to poor air quality on buses and the length of time they are subjected to it; in fact, "while it receives little attention, in-car air pollution may pose one of the greatest modern threats to human health" (15, 17). Obviously, the pursuit of educational outcomes should not be carried out to the detriment of a student's health. Keeping schools within the local community, working towards shorter bus rides, and encouraging active transportation, rather than eliminating the opportunity, should be a common mandate when planning for schools.

Buses must often travel over badly maintained roads and in poor weather conditions. There are also serious concerns when children aged four to eighteen ride together in an environment that is essentially unsupervised. Crude language, bullying, drug use, and inappropriate touching are all noted in anecdotal reports. Since the release of the Nova Scotia report of the Task Force on Bullying and Cyberbullying in February 2012 by Wayne MacKay, curbing the alarming incidence of bullying in and around schools has been a provincial policy priority. Allowing rural schools to close and forcing elementary students, ages four to ten, to ride on school buses for two to three hours per day flies directly in the face of this initiative.

Long bus rides also devalue and consume inordinate amounts of children's time (Howley, Howley and Shamblen 2001). Students who travel two hours per day to school spend forty hours per month in an environment which is neither productive nor recreational, and they are not compensated for their travel time. How many adults would accept this situation for themselves? Perhaps the most harmful effect of busing is the message sent to rural children: "Your community cannot give you what you need, and you must go 'down the road' for your education." It's a message that perpetuates a mindset that rural communities represent a dead end — that children must leave in order to thrive.

The Quality of Education

"School consolidation has often been achieved by over-riding public opinion on the basis of claims about the educational and financial benefits of larger schools. These alleged benefits are not supported by any significant evidence, and the more researchers have looked at the question of school size, the more clear it becomes that small schools are actually superior." — Michael Corbett and Dennis Mulcahy, *Education on a Human Scale: Small Rural Schools in a Modern Context* (2006)

School consolidations cannot be said to improve the quality of education in the Nova Scotian context; in fact, the opposite is true. Closing small rural schools actually erodes the quality of education for most rural students (Corbett and Mulcahy 2006). Longer bus rides affect children's ability to attend in the classroom, interfere with the time they have to do homework, and may discourage high school students from taking more challenging classes. In addition, students lose the well-documented advantages of the small school (and sometimes multi-age) learning environment when they are sent to larger schools outside of their communities. For economically disadvantaged children and children with specific learning profiles, in particular, small community schools present a distinct advantage (Truscott and Truscott 2005). School research indicates that children bused to schools over long distances often have less access to extracurricular activities. Small, community schools are more likely to provide all learners with opportunities to get involved — which is important as a number of studies link student participation to likelihood of graduation (Cotton 1996; Corbett and Mulcahy 2006). There is also a loss to the education system as a whole when small, rural schools are closed. These vibrant, community-connected, nurturing environments are often leaders in parental involvement, student engagement, multi-age learning, and innovative teaching, whose successes should be studied and emulated.

Parent–Community Involvement

"The size of the school and its proximity and connection to the students' home communities is a crucial factor in creating a quality school." — Michael Corbett and Dennis Mulcahy, *Education on a Human Scale: Small Rural Schools in a Modern Context* (2006)

Nova Scotia's Kids and Learning First strategy places appropriate emphasis on strengthening the links between schools, parents, and the community. The irony is that those links are arguably strongest in small, rural schools — the very schools that are under constant threat of closure. Parents in these schools tend to report excellent communication with teachers and a high degree of involvement in the school (Corbett and Mulcahy 2006). Parents, community members, teachers, and students feel like family, and there are fewer issues with bullying and discipline. The result is an enriched and enriching environment where learning flows organically beyond the walls of the classroom and into the wider community.

When rural schools close, parents and communities feel bereft — not for nostalgic reasons but because that deep and immediate connection to the children and the school is lost. Parents may find it more difficult to participate

Six boys attending Weymouth Consolidated School pose before the Public Hearing in March 2012. Hand-made signs delivered an unmistakable message — spare our school. (Photo: Karla Kelly)

at a school in another community and may be less connected to their child's education. The community loses the ability to foster its young, to pass on community traditions, and to share cultural heritage.

Short-Term Costs

"Even though people may appreciate the benefits of small schools, too many think that the cost of such schools is prohibitive.... Measuring the cost of education by graduates rather than by all students who go through the system suggests that small schools are a wise investment.... Small schools are not prohibitively expensive. Investing tax dollars in small schools does make sense." — Barbara Kent Lawrence et al., *Dollars & Sense: The Cost Effectiveness of Small Schools* (2002), p. viii

Can small schools be built cost effectively and does investing in small schools make financial sense? Those are critical questions, even for those who see the tremendous benefits of small schools for children, parents, and families in Nova Scotia's rural communities. These questions are also germane to those who harbour the opinion that small schools are prohibitively expensive because they are half-empty, visibly older in appearance, and often poorly maintained by school boards. Among those skeptics are facilities planners and board staff who believe that spending money to keep small schools open is wasteful.

New research findings point in a completely different direction. When small schools are viewed as community assets rather than school board liabilities, the whole equation looks much different. On annual operating costs alone, small schools like Petite Elementary and Weymouth Consolidated, are cheaper to operate per square foot of space. A small school like Petite Riviere Elementary costs 4.75 dollars per square foot to operate (including custodial, heat, electricity, snow, and garbage removal), compared to an average of $6 per foot, or 20 percent more, for a new super-sized elementary school (Helmer 2013).

For those who prefer to view schools as more than floor space, small schools are usually more cost effective on a cost per graduate basis. Small schools tend to boost academic achievement, as well as achieve higher retention and graduation rates. An American study found that high school costs for graduates at smaller schools ($49,553) are marginally less than at larger schools ($49,578). The main factor was retention rates, since fewer small school students drop out of high school (Lawrence et al. 2002: 11–12).

Closing schools and abandoning buildings also has cost implications for local taxpayers. While the school board can unload unwanted properties, they revert to the local municipalities. In the case of the Municipality of Lunenburg, it has cost taxpayers $75,000 a year to keep three abandoned schools (Riverport, Centre Consolidated, and Blockhouse) on idle, awaiting disposition or demolition. It will cost thousands more to demolish them, a likely scenario for one or more of these cast-off schools (Helmer 2013). The costs of disposal are ultimately borne by the same local taxpayers.

Long-Term Costs

"Many rural areas in… Atlantic Canada face a number of challenges that impact on educational decision-making. These include out-migration, declining birth rate, declining school enrollment, and economic challenges of various kinds. Closing and consolidation of small schools should not be seen as a solution to these challenges. The research would appear to indicate that small schools offer the children of these rural communities the best chance of success." — Michael Corbett and Dennis Mulcahy, *Education on a Human Scale: Small Rural Schools in a Modern Context* (2006)

Closing rural schools in order to reduce Nova Scotia Education expenditures is beginning to look more and more like a false economy. While impact assessment reports purport to demonstrate that some savings can be made by closing schools and reducing maintenance costs, those perceived gains are generally negated when the loss of "social capital" and costs in terms of community health, economic development, and student achievement are taken into account.

School closures and consolidations do not always bring financial savings, and school consolidations in Nova Scotia during the mid 1990s did not result in more money for public schools (Corbett and Mulcahy 2006). As fuel prices continue to rise, it makes sense to question whether busing children farther from their communities to larger facilities will be as cost effective as keeping children in small schools close to home, especially when you factor in the long term health, environmental, and social costs associated with busing. Furthermore, the official cost estimates for new and larger schools never include all the infrastructure costs associated with those schools, such as roads, sidewalks, signage, lights, and additional policing.

There may also be hidden health costs related to rural school closures. A Middlesex-London Health Unit report, prepared by Graham L. Pollett, MD, in October 2008, took an initial look at the health and safety effects of long bus rides. It identified links between school bus time and physical activity, safety, bullying, air quality, and academic performance (Pollett 2008). Although more research in this area is needed, anecdotal reports suggest a

Historic Bass River Elementary School is a typical example of the impact of deferred maintenance. After letting schools deteriorate for five or ten years, it's much easier to mount a case for school closure to save on renovation costs. (Private collection)

link between the loss of community schools and increased rates of stress and anxiety in rural families. Bus fumes constitute a major pollutant in rural areas. Serious concerns have been raised about air quality in school buses, and experts like Catherine O'Brien of Cape Breton University have claimed that not reducing children's exposure to pollutants in these vehicles could be more costly in the long run (O'Brien 2008: 15). Longer hours spent on the bus translate into fewer opportunities for active, healthy living and are linked to higher rates of obesity (Ecology Action Centre 2011).

Small, community schools are more likely to produce students who graduate from high school and secure better careers. A New York University Education Institute study (1998) found that small schools were more expensive on a short-tem cost-per-student basis; however, when viewed on the basis of the number of students they graduated, they were less expensive in the long run. A Nebraska study in 1999 demonstrated that the so-called "inefficiencies of small schools" are greatly reduced when calculated on the basis of cost per graduate and are negligible when the social costs of dropouts and the benefits of producing college-educated citizens are factored into the equation (see also Funk and Bailey 1999: 1; Lawrence et al. 2002: 11).

Most disturbingly, the closure of rural schools profoundly affects a community's viability. Two key American studies, undertaken in Minnesota and New York, assessed the social and economic impact of school closures on rural communities. School consolidations in six Minnesota counties and in upstate New York have resulted in economic fallout in terms of loss of tax-paying citizens and reduction in area retail sales (Sederberg 1987: 125–30; Lyson 2002). In communities with boarded-up schools, the evidence is plainly visible: "For Sale" signs sprout on front lawns. Families move away, fewer families settle in the area, professionals and entrepreneurs make financial investments elsewhere.

In rural Nova Scotia communities, the loss of the school can sound a death knell for a village or small town. Indeed, rural school closures have come to seem, for many, like the primary weapon in an unwritten policy to depopulate the countryside and move rural dwellers into the cities. A government that is truly committed to enabling a thriving rural population must place rural children and their education at the forefront. Creative partnerships with communities that are already deeply involved in their schools can ensure that healthy, vibrant rural schools can come out from under the threat of closure and take their rightful place as the centrepiece of rural revitalization.

4

The Turnaround Strategy
From School Closures to Rural Revitalization

"I believe that every school board in the province would be happy to see the government review that legislation…. It's stressful for the community and it's certainly challenging for the school board because I don't know any school board member that would want to close out any services in any community…. It's not a very positive process. It's one, I think, that should be looked at to see if there's a better way of doing this." — Mary Jess MacDonald, Chair, Strait Regional School Board, *CBC News Nova Scotia*, March 9, 2012.

"The Magic School Bus, that children's series about travelling through space and time, might provide us with a starting point. It might be possible to imagine contemporary small, rural schools as vibrant educational sites … critical to the prosperity of their communities and providing high quality schools for children." — Michael Corbett, "The Magic Bus." Address to Small Schools Summit, January 2012, NSCC, Bridgewater

After the restoration of the school review process in September 2009, school closures continued under a new set of legalistic rules that formalized a process pitting school boards against the communities they purport to serve. The rules of engagement were clarified in 2008 and the impact assessment reports are more consistent and reliable, but they still reflect the priorities of facilities planners rather than those of parents seeking quality education for their children. With school enrollments declining, particularly in rural areas, the school review process became a regulated, quasi-judicial "chopping block" on the road to a more consolidated, regionalized, and remote school system. Stopping the closure process is only the first step — opening the door to developing a rural turnaround strategy both province-wide and at the level of the community school. Today provincial strategies abound for every conceivable ill afflicting Nova Scotia, so the litmus test is what impact such a policy would actually have on children, teachers, and families.

The school review process seems to be dying a slow death. Defenders of the legislated process contend that it does not always lead to closure, so it can be a vehicle for promoting school improvement. If that is the real purpose, there are many better alternatives than putting whole school communities through the wringer. Schools identified for review are given notice that they are being considered for closure. That does not send a school improvement message, and it puts school boards and school communities on a collision course. Being granted a reprieve is all most small, rural schools can hope for under the draconian provincial school review system.

School boards too find the school review process not only grueling but terribly divisive and damaging to school-community relations. Gradually, it has dawned on school board superintendents that it was, ultimately, a losing proposition, leaving elected board members psychologically battered and bruised and small school advocates either enraged or barely mollified by hastily arranged facilities-driven compromises. Whether it was in the Strait Region, the Tri-County Region, or the Halifax Region, the prolonged school review process simply proved to be a damaging one for schools, boards, and communities. Staunch defenders of the process eventually resorted to arguing either that school boards had no other option or that it was "too late" to revisit past decisions.

Suspending the School Closure Process

The chair of the Strait Regional School Board, Mary Jess MacDonald, was one of the first to give voice to her angst and unease. After presiding over a process that recommended shuttering three schools in March 2012 (West Richmond Education Centre in Evanston, Rev. H.J. MacDonald in Heatherton, and Canso Academy in Canso), she publicly called for changes to the school review process.

Provincial governments in Nova Scotia certainly have the power to change the rules of the game for small schools and rural communities. Simply stepping back and allowing school boards to conduct round after round of "school accommodation" reviews is wreaking havoc on rural communities and undermining support for public education. Opening of new "big box" schools like Bluenose Academy or building new school additions amounts to "buying-off a minority" and applying a temporary healing ointment to the long-term wounds done to a small town, village, or rural school district.

Provincial education ministers have always had the authority to declare a moratorium on the school review process, an option exercised in March 2006 by Jamie Muir. The pretext then was to secure sufficient time to assess the fairness of the review process. Today, the situation is far more acute. The revamped school review process did not improve the situation and continued to chew-up rural communities, abandoning groups of families willing to

The village of Bass River turns out in force in January 2010 for the public hearing held at West Colchester Consolidated School to review the case for closure of Bass River School. Spared the axe in February 2010, it was slated for closure in June 2013, its hundredth anniversary year. (Private collection)

stand up and fight for local community access to our public schools. It's time to permanently suspend the process of foreclosure. That is why the Small Schools Initiative delegation has campaigned for a moratorium on all school reviews and the rolling back of decisions made in the last two rounds of school closures. We have always contended that a cessation for a minimum of one year would allow the minister and the Department to take the lead in developing a Schools at the Centre rural revitalization strategy, in collaboration with Economic and Rural Development and other provincial authorities.

Calling a halt to the school review process brings immediate relief to schools threatened with closure. That is, of course, only a half measure — and it will only prove transitory unless it is followed-up with a new public engagement strategy changing the whole dynamic from "threatened closures" to community-based, school-centred, rural economic and social development.

The Critical Need for a Rural Revitalization Strategy

As the rural population of Nova Scotia continues to decline, so do the programs and services offered to rural citizens. Over the years, too many communities have watched businesses, churches, hospitals, and government offices slowly disappear. And, too often, the youth of these communities follow in search of a way to make a living, leaving behind little room for economic growth and opportunity. Often the school is the last community service left, and this is why so many communities fight so hard to keep their schools.

In its disturbing 2008 report on rural poverty, *Beyond Freefall*, the Senate Standing Committee on Agriculture and Forestry summed the core issue up with clarity and precision: "In rural Canada, schools are more than just places where children and youth earn an education. They are also the hub and lifeblood of the community. When the local school goes, all too often so does the community" (Senate of Canada 2008). Recognizing the important role a school plays in a community in terms of attracting and retaining a population base, and therefore contributing to the economic viability and growth of the community, the question remains: Why does the antiquated trend of removing schools from our communities continue?

The answer is simple — there is a lack of support for rural communities in Nova Scotia and furthermore a lack of government-driven strategic planning and policy development that addresses the needs of rural families and the education of their children. This is evident in the following comment expressed by the Nova Scotia School Board Association (NSSBA) in the School Closure Process Review Committee Report and Recommendations (2009): "The school board's primary responsibility is public school program delivery, not rural economic development." The two items, of course, are not mutually exclusive of one another. This narrow vision of the role of such an important agency reflects the difficulties faced when different agencies work in uncoordinated ways or even counter to one another. Nova Scotia's Economic and Rural Development Department puts money into the Regional Development Authorities (RDAs) to facilitate community re-development, while the school board in that same region closes the local school, one of the community's most important pieces of infrastructure.

The Nova Scotia government has an opportunity to solve this problem. Communities across the province are upset and frustrated with the threat of school closures as they continue to fight for their schools and their communities. Budget cuts may be inevitable, but with adequate time taken for research, planning, and strategy development, this government could become a visionary leader in Nova Scotia's education history with the first ever strategy for rural education and sustainability. The result would be a province embracing its rural citizens, promoting rural viability through education and economic growth and attracting young people back to a province where rural life can provide an equitable level of programs and services.

The rural population of Nova Scotia (living outside centres of 5,000 or more people) accounts for 45 percent of the overall population. These citizens not only deserve equitable services, but they have the knowledge and expertise to help bring Nova Scotia in line with other provinces that are stepping up, listening to their rural citizens, engaging them in dialogue, and meeting their needs with visionary policies and innovative technological advancements.

The voices of some 425,450 rural Nova Scotians are important and vital to policy development, and they should be heard.

A coordinated, strategic approach to rural education and sustainability is imperative to the future of Nova Scotia. This is exactly the kind of strategy that many other provinces and territories have put in place to ensure equitable programs and services for their rural residents. A few excerpts from these rural strategies, extracted from government policies and research papers, provide insight into the foresight and strategic thinking evident in other parts of the country.

Manitoba

Collaboration among school divisions, the provincial Government and community agencies is essential to the articulation and implementation of effective strategies and actions which will ensure a high quality of educational opportunity for all students in rural and remote areas of our province. (*Rural Education in Manitoba: Defining Challenges, Creating Solutions*, 2002: 5)

Alberta

As part of Alberta's plan, a Minister's Advisory Committee on Small and Rural School Programming was to be established along with "incentives … to encourage rural school jurisdictions and educational institutions to work with community agencies to make their schools and facilities a hub of services for children, communities and lifelong learning. (*A Place to Grow Alberta's Rural Development Strategy*, Executive Summary, 2005)

Ontario

Our plan for rural Ontario recognizes that when young people have access to good education in local schools, our communities can grow stronger. (*Ontario's Rural Plan Update 2006*)

Prince Edward Island

Given that many people prefer a rural lifestyle, rural communities that offer comparable levels of connectivity and educational services will soon be able to compete with urban centres for residents with high-quality talent and expertise, especially those communities with a vibrant local culture and identity. If rural communities can attract, and retain, even a small percentage of people seeking to raise their families in a rural environment — whether they earn their living in the community or an urban centre — these citizens could provide rural Prince Edward Island with the economic foundation it needs to maintain its way of life and achieve a higher quality of life. (*Rural Action Plan: A Rural Economic Development Strategy for Prince Edward Island*, 2010)

While the Nova Scotia government does have a Department of Economic and Rural Development and Tourism and the Department of Education's new *Kids and Learning First* plan, these in no way constitute the kind of strategic thinking and integrated planning necessary to tackle the issues of rural education, rural depopulation, and rural economics, not to mention the most basic right of any child — a quality educational experience within her or his own community.

The government has various separate programs in place targeting the rural population, such as Broadband for Rural Nova Scotia (BRNS), SchoolsPlus, and the Small Isolated Schools Supplement. Unfortunately, a lack of alignment in interdepartmental policies and the absence of an overall vision for rural Nova Scotia places these programs in silos where they do not have the opportunity to complement each other. Why does a government on one hand remove schools from rural communities (which results in families moving away, limiting the potential for newcomers, and strengthening the further decline of the rural economy), and at the same time promote rural economic development with initiatives such as BRNS? If Nova Scotia wants families to prosper and remain in rural communities, their essential needs must be met with an integrated, coordinated approach. This obviously includes education.

Developing and pursuing a rural strategy in education is not unknown in Nova Scotia, The construction of district high schools from the 1940s until the 1960s, as Michael Corbett and Dennis Mulcahy point out, was "in itself a mechanism for finally including rural people in the public secondary system." More recently, that same "inclusion project" has been broadened to address what they describe as "multiple layers of disadvantage including gender, race, and social class inequality. What is odd is that living in a rural area is now a geographic disadvantage that is not being addressed, particularly in education, health care, and community services (Corbett and Mulcahy 2006). Being poor and living in a rural place is tantamount to a double disadvantage in contemporary Nova Scotia.

Rural Nova Scotians are again becoming a disenfranchised group facing discrimination and being provided with second-rate services. In previous cycles of decline, rural citizens have been underserved and have watched institutions leave their communities with little rationalization or justification. "Each level of government," according to Corbett and Mulcahy, "seems to understand that this is wrong and that the historical power imbalance and failure to include rural people in decision-making has not generally produced good outcomes" (Corbett and Mulcahy 2006). Recognizing the problem is one thing, taking meaningful action quite another.

Some 80 percent of the students attending the Chignecto-Central Regional School Board public schools are bused to school each day. Here the yellow buses prepare to take the children home at Great Village School, Great Village, Colchester County. (Private collection)

A rural development strategy for Nova Scotia must not only set out a clear, coherent direction, but also be flexible enough to respond to the unique characteristics of the various regions. Setting provincial priorities will be crucial to the success of initiatives aimed at securing longer-term sustainability, stimulating entrepreneurship, fostering local innovation, and reducing socio-economic disparities. The Coastal Communities Network got it right in their March 2009 report on Rural Development Assessment. A provincial strategy must, above all, in the words of Dennis Pilkey, "address the need for stronger supports for community-led development efforts appropriate to rural Nova Scotia." With the education system divided up into eight regional school board territories, promoting a "community-centred approach" can be difficult. Consistency of purpose is paramount, but it must also be flexible and adaptable enough to meet the unique needs of communities as diverse as Maitland, Lunenburg, Canso, and Middle River.

The community-based approach favoured by Nova Scotia's Coastal Communities Network is remarkably consistent with that informing *Reversing the Tide*, British Columbia's 2009 policy initiative. "Rural policy must resolve an important conundrum in delivering rural development programs," the B.C. document astutely observes. "In an era of enormous fiscal stress, one transcending demand for rural policy will be finding the most efficient way possible to deliver critical development programs. At the same time, by its very nature, the new rural paradigm marks the end of the one-size-fits-all policy era. This means programs must be flexible and tailored to the unique needs of every region" (Government of British Columbia 2009).

Rural communities are uniquely situated to provide a real life education for children. One of the five key principles set out in the 2008 Senate report *Beyond Freefall* is that policies and practices adopted by rural communities and institutions should reflect and respect local ways, traditions, and practices. Departments of education and school boards promoting standardized or "one-size-fits-all" curricula, programs, and services cut against the grain of rural and small town life. The Senate report, once again, put it best: "Place-based thinking puts emphasis on the idea that local people can come up with local solutions that capitalize on local assets and local enthusiasm. The role of higher levels of government, as stressed in our interim report, must be to facilitate and not dictate policy" (Senate of Canada 2008).

Having a rural education and sustainability strategy matters because it articulates a vision and tends to attract resources to advance the rural regeneration agenda. Strategy development is a time-consuming process which involves research, needs analysis, community engagement, and partnership development. We have the recent experience and expertise of the Coastal Communities Network to draw upon in moving from talk to action (Pilkey 2009: 42–43). It is hard work, but it has a big payoff. By not only consulting, but also engaging the players involved, the government has an opportunity to draw on the great wealth of information and expertise which exists throughout the province — within its citizen base and within other levels of government. This is an opportunity and a resource not to be overlooked when beginning such an exercise.

A rural strategy would set clear goals and benchmarks to measure our progress toward building more sustainable, healthier, and better educated rural communities. "Evergreening" rural Nova Scotia will have real benefits for everyone. Saving small rural schools is only the beginning because to survive the next school review they must be transformed into true community hub schools. With secure public schools, communities are much better placed to gain economic ground and develop a renewed sense of confidence in future viability (Lyson 2002). It will take time, energy, and perseverance, but slowly the villages and towns will resume growing and attracting new families and businesses so critical to rural sustainability.

Once a rural strategy is in place, the real work begins for Nova Scotians. System-wide proclamations mean little without a revitalization at the school and community level. Just as rural areas continue to be marginalized in a globalized, networked, and centrally managed education state, rural schools and their children get lost on the radar. Formal education, as Nova Scotia

Liberal MLA Junior Theriault aptly observed a decade ago, leads far too often to "outmigration in coastal communities" (Corbett 2004). Children and youth in Digby Neck, for example, have reported for years that schooling in rural fishing villages means, in Michael Corbett's turn-of-phrase, "learning to leave." For that to change will require the introduction of a new rural, place-based curriculum, attuned to the interests of rural children, and the training and recruitment of teachers capable of embracing what is termed an "education for sustainability" in rural and small town Nova Scotia (Corbett 2006: 291; Boon 2011). It will require major reform and binary action, combining an overall strategy with school-community level innovation and reform.

5

Rural Strategy
and Curriculum Reform
The Building Blocks

"While many rural communities are experiencing a decline in population ... declining populations do not make the people remaining there any less deserving. We must find innovative, creative ways to deliver high-quality social programs and services in our rural communities." — *Weaving the Threads: A Lasting Social Fabric,* Nova Scotia Department of Community Services, (revised 2010)

Expanding Online Learning in Rural Communities: "Triple the number of students (from 500 to 1,500) who can take on-line courses through Nova Scotia's virtual school." — Nova Scotia Education, *Kids and Learning First* (February 2012) p. 16

Calls for rural revitalization and economic regeneration are not really new in Nova Scotia. Since its inception in January 2012, the Nova Scotia Small Schools Initiative has carried forward and built upon the foundational work done by earlier grassroots groups like the Coastal Communities Network (CCN). That earlier initiative was spawned by the 1991 collapse of the ground fishery, an economic shock that touched every aspect of every coastal community: schools, churches, businesses. Right across Nova Scotia, many people were left wondering if the coastal way of life would soon disappear as well. Out of that adversity was born a fierce determination to take up the fight for community survival. That was over fifteen years ago, and today the struggle continues on a new battleground — saving small schools and rural communities threatened by the latest incursion of a centralizing, bureaucratic education state.

The Coastal Communities Network blazed the path and pointed the province in the direction of building sustainable rural communities (RCIPP 2003). Working outside the formal structures and the system, it attempted to bridge the gulf separating the public and voluntary sectors, bringing together groups that traditionally did not work with each other. Communities, government, organizations, and institutions were encouraged to identify thorny

Rural Policy Forum: The Coastal Communities Network held Rural Policy Forums in 2006 and 2007 which focused on giving expression to rural concerns, in addition to holding monthly Learning Circles/Clusters and providing research reports on critical issues. (Photo: CCN and Mark Austin)

issues, influence policy, and generate ideas. Eventually, the CCN branched out to include non-coastal rural communities as well. A CCN study of the economic impact of wharves in the province demonstrated that, by 2002, fish exports had reached $1.2 billion, placing Nova Scotia first in Canada for fish exports.

The CCN called itself the Large Voice for rural Nova Scotia and played an instrumental role in forging partnerships across Nova Scotia and in the United States, working closely with the American Rural Policy Research Institute. Taking a practical, common sense approach earned the CCN accolades and acceptance within government ranks, most notably within the Nova Scotia Office of Economic Development (2005) and the Gulf of Maine Council on the Marine Environment (2006). The CCN is well connected with provincial tourism ventures and, in particular, is popular with boaters as it produced a wharf-by-wharf profile of the entire province showing where to land and dock and what facilities, such as restaurants, bathrooms, and fresh water are near by.

The CCN's greatest contribution was the development of Community Counts for the Nova Scotia government. Based upon the Canadian Census of 2006, Dr. Dennis Pilkey and his team constructed a "snapshot of Nova Scotia," providing accurate, detailed, and invaluable statistical data on each community across the province (Nova Scotia N.D.). It was initiated by the CCN through the Rural Communities Impacting Policy Project, a partnership with the Atlantic Health Promotion Research Centre at Dalhousie University. While the Community Counts website is an invaluable information tool, especially for Nova Scotia municipalities and businesses, it has never been exploited to its full potential. The experiment proved that providing community development tools was only half the battle. Without inspired leadership, innovative ideas, and capacity-building, great tools go underutilized and are vulnerable to budget cuts.

What lessons can be learned from the Coastal Communities Network story? Launched with passion and fierce determination, the CCN provides a cautionary tale in the struggle for social reform and systemic change. Building partnerships and working with governments can become all consuming and mutate into endless capacity-building efforts. Holding monthly "Learning Circles" may well be unique to Nova Scotia, but they tend to generate more talk about "wind power, water quality, labour trends, and climate change" while diffusing the creative conflict that is needed for system change. Projects like CCN's On Common Ground are worthwhile, building greater understanding among African Nova Scotian, Mi'kmaq, Acadian, and other European groups in Nova Scotia, but they are low impact. Since 2011, the Network has been renamed the Rural & Coastal Communities Network and is now led by new executive director Mark Austin, a resident of Old Barns, Colchester County. For all of its ups and downs, the RCCN may well be poised for a breakthrough. With Austin serving as research director of the Nova Scotia Commission on the New Economy, you can expect his home agency to get a new lease on life. This much is certain: without a fire in the belly, it's easy to be absorbed into the existing political and economic order in Nova Scotia.

The future looks threatening for rural education and community life. Departure and loss have been continuing themes for rural Nova Scotians since the 1940s. Children raised in small towns, on farms, or in fishing villages have been leaving their rural communities in droves, lured by better employment prospects elsewhere. Until recently, the role that the school system played had been widely discussed but little studied. That changed with the publication of Michael Corbett's *Learning to Leave* (2007a), a groundbreaking book providing a detailed study of schooling and social mobility in a Maritime coastal community, Digby Neck, Nova Scotia.

From 1997 until 2001, Corbett pursued a deceptively simple research question: "In this coastal community, who stays, who goes, and why?" His study begins and ends with a troubling ambivalence spawned by the irony of, and contradictions in, rural schooling. For most rural youth in Digby Neck, schooling meant "learning to leave" and a passport out of rural Nova Scotia. Rather than building and supporting communities, Corbett revealed a system of public schooling that may actually contribute to rural depopulation and decline. Standardized curriculum, programs, and tests at odds with rural sensibilities, in his words, "render schools irrelevant for large numbers of young people attending schools in rural, northern, and coastal communities" (Corbett 2007a: 3–5, 72–103).

Corbett's case study has profound implications for Nova Scotians. If Digby Neck is representative of the rural experience, public schooling, especially in regional high schools, can be an alienating experience for rural youth. Acquiring book learning and securing a diploma provides greater educational mobility that, paradoxically, disconnects them from their homes and families. For most of those left behind, formal education is considered "an alien, impractical, and progressively abstract space." We are presented with a conundrum. If today's rural education is really about assisting youth to leave, then policies ought to "support transitions for rural youth and their communities." If not, then public schooling ought to respond to the needs of the majority who prefer to "remain close to home in places that stubbornly refuse to die." While it might be wishful thinking, Corbett suggested that schools explore ways of meeting the needs of both the leavers and the stay-at-homes (243–73).

Rebuilding rural Nova Scotia starts with taking the pulse of the community and checking its vital signs. Small towns and inland communities like Lunenburg County on the South Shore provide a point of entry into the current and future state of education in rural Nova Scotia. Back in 2010, the South Shore Regional School Board was planning to close the Town of Lunenburg's high school and to bus the students across the county. In the midst of the debate, the School Board was presented with a troubling set of findings calling into question the wisdom of closing the town's only high school. The *Lunenburg County Vital Signs* report, produced by the Lunenburg County Community Fund (2010) found that traditional jobs were disappearing, the population under age thirty-four was decreasing, and this rural area was not doing well with respect to the education-acquired skills necessary to meet the demands of the new community and the new economy.

Educational levels in Lunenburg County were a major cause for concern, even in one of Nova Scotia's South Shore tourist havens. In 2009, in the Southern Nova Scotia Economic Region (which includes Lunenburg County), only 67.0 percent of the population aged fifteen years and older had completed high school. This rate was 11.0 percent below the provincial rate of 75.3 percent, and 15.2 percent below the national rate of 79.0 percent. Fewer still went on to post-secondary education, even though the Nova Scotia Community College, Bridgewater Campus, was reasonably close to the district's high schools. Indeed, the *Vital Signs* study reported that only 45.2 percent of the population had completed post-secondary education (university degree, post-secondary certificate, or diploma), a rate 10.1 percent *below* the provincial average of 50.3 percent and 11.0 percent *below* the national average of 50.8 percent. Most significantly, more than half, or 53 percent, of the total labour force in Lunenburg County does not have any post-secondary education (Lunenburg County Community Fund 2010).

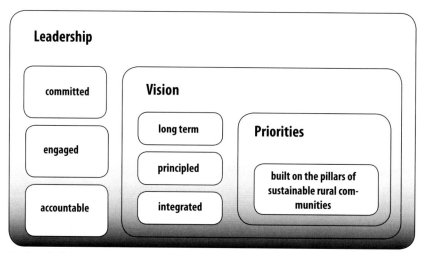

A schematic diagram produced by Sandra Labor for the Schools at the Centre report, May 15, 2012.

Faced with this disturbing evidence, the school board remained undeterred and closed the town's only high school, adding two more hours to a student's high school day. Such is the appeal of school consolidation for the sake of saving a few dollars and balancing the budget. It's also a recipe for further depopulating a small town in rural Nova Scotia.

The closure of Lunenburg's local high school is part of a much larger story repeated over and over again, in town after town, village after village. No wonder rural Nova Scotians are asking for a stronger voice and leadership in the decision-making around the schools, programs, and services that are necessary to keep their communities alive and sustainable for the future. In spite of the valiant efforts of the Coastal Communities Network since 1991, rural Nova Scotia is slowly closing down before our eyes. A comprehensive rural strategy is needed in order to protect the rural quality of life, support the populations that live there, and enhance the economic opportunities that are constantly changing within a globalized and information driven world.

There is no need to completely re-invent the wheel. Many other Canadian provinces have taken the lead on committing to the value of their rural areas, and we can learn from their experience. In all cases, it is recognized that meeting the challenges and needs in rural communities requires a coordinated, interconnected strategy based on the principles of what makes a sustainable rural community.

The building blocks in developing a rural strategy for Nova Scotia were identified in a remarkable little report entitled *Rural Education: A School and Community Partnership*, produced in 2009 by Sandra Labor and a Parent Focus Group at Shatford Memorial Elementary School in Hubbards, N.S. Building upon that initial research, Sandra give a presentation at the Small

Schools Summit held in Bridgewater in January 2012 and then developed a pro-active approach to creating and advancing a rural revitalization strategy for Nova Scotia.

Leadership

A committed leadership must be present at all levels, from the local community through to provincial departments. A successful rural strategy requires community-based models of engagement that build on the unique assets and strengths of community members, along with municipal and provincial planners, as are transparent accountability and information sharing at all levels. The rural plans for both Ontario and Alberta reflect a commitment to develop strategies directly with communities. Ontario's rural plan notes that "real progress ... has to be a team effort. Together with communities, municipalities, businesses and citizens working in partnership, we can ensure a bright future for rural Ontario while staying fiscally responsible" (Ontario Ministry of Municipal Affairs and Housing 2004, 2006).

Tapping into the talents and energies of grassroots groups is critical to a rural strategy's success. Alberta established the Rural Alberta Citizens' Voice, a representative group of people from rural Alberta which provides advice to the minister of agriculture, food and rural development (Government of Alberta 2005). At the community level, Sandra Labor's small rural school in Hubbards, Nova Scotia, took the initiative in 2009 to create their own strategic planning document in order to strengthen their viability for the future. Such grassroots resources can offer a springboard for new models of community engagement and leadership around schools.

Imagining a Larger Vision

Developing a broader vision is critical to transforming the silo-ed departments housed within the Nova Scotia government. While different government departments and levels of government have statements related to the value of our rural populations, Nova Scotia does not have a clearly articulated vision. As a result, different tiers of government work within their own mandates without envisioning a "bigger picture." We continue to see well-meaning policies in one department contradicting the direction of another.

We need a vision for rural Nova Scotia that imagines the future possibilities of our rural communities, recognizing that technology is vastly changing how businesses and services are able to function. We need a long-term strategy with a set of core principles that guide the planning by all interested parties.

Setting Rural Development Priorities

After defining an overall vision for rural Nova Scotia, the next step is to decide upon the essential components of a sustainable rural community and identify the priorities necessary to reflect these. This cannot be a top-down process but rather one demonstrating a true commitment to public engagement. In order to authenticate this whole process, rural citizens must be involved in defining these priorities.

Sustainability requires paying close attention to the integration and balancing of social, economic, environmental, and cultural well-being factors when making decisions. Nova Scotia has already begun the process of defining such priorities through its Sustainable Communities Initiative, developed in 1999. The initiative's purpose was to support communities through a coordinated approach that integrated social, cultural, economic, and environmental policies and programs. The SCI vision was for communities and governments to work together toward long term sustainability. We could find no evidence of the implementation or continuation of this initiative since 2004.

The Nova Scotia Social Prosperity Framework also acknowledges that "social prosperity, economic prosperity, and environmental sustainability are linked and depend on each other, and as such, efforts in these three areas must also weave together in a way that supports sustainable prosperity and self-reliance, within the New Nova Scotia" (Nova Scotia Government 2010).

There is no need to re-invent the wheel. Alberta's rural plan identifies 1) economic growth; 2) community capacity, quality of life and infrastructure; 3) health care, and 4) learning and skill development as the four pillars essential for sustainable rural communities. Ontario's rural plan identifies strong people, strong economy, better health, and success for students as the priorities.

Education has tremendous untapped potential to be a vehicle for renewed sustainability in Nova Scotia's rural communities. Just as learning for the twenty-first century requires innovation, creativity, adaptability, and collaboration, these skills need to be applied to the challenges met by rural communities. With sustainable rural communities as the overriding goal, we need to adapt to different ways of thinking about the buildings that facilitate the public school program. Much of the current research leans towards the idea of a multi-service building to reduce the overhead cost of delivering public education. Premier Darrell Dexter, while fulfilling the role of opposition leader, was quoted as recognizing that "pulling undervalued schools from some rural communities is like pulling threads from a blanket. It makes the fabric very, very thin ... [we need] to look for ways schools can deliver compatible new services" (*Chronicle-Herald*, March 2006: A6).

This broader thinking is echoed in Dawn C. Wallin's 2009 nationwide

Review of Provincial and Territorial Initiatives for Rural Education. Surveying best practice in rural schooling, she wrote:

> Rural schools have become more sophisticated and more adept at doing what they have always done best — they rely on the local expertise and the concept of community to work together with partners in order to find ways to innovate, to offer as many opportunities as they can for the students they serve, and to support the local people who work hard to make sure their children receive the best education they have to offer. [What works best?] A symbiotic relationship [based on] mutually beneficial, equitable and authentic partnerships; strategic direction and planning at both the grass roots and provincial/territorial levels. (2)

Creating those synergies only comes through genuine two-way exchanges and mutually supportive relationships, exemplified in the grassroots community schools movement.

Networked School Communities

Driven by the realization that education is no longer constrained by physical parameters, new types of schooling are emerging. The term "isolated" has taken on a meaning that primarily refers to geographic location. Children are now connected to the global community no matter where they physically reside. A school can now be many things, allowing greater diversity and flexibility in delivering educational outcomes. Exciting conversations are happening in rural and small town Nova Scotia about the potential for transforming small schools into genuine community hubs. This is based on the assumption that the facility that delivers education within a rural community is most efficient and effective when other services are combined in the same location. Some of these ideas are being sparked by innovative thinking in the United States. Small school advocates have ready online access to vitally important sources, such as Joe Nathan and Karen Febey's 2002 book, *Smaller, Saner Successful Schools*, which offers twenty-two examples from around the United States of schools that have made partnerships with their communities in ways that help each become more sustainable (Lawrence et al. 2002).

The rural social and economic landscape has drastically changed with the advent of technology. Just as small technology "start-up" firms are sprouting up in the North American business world, so are the first generation of networked, community-based rural schools. Most children and families now have Internet access and are connected to the global community no matter where they live. The Innovation Lab Schools, initiated in the MidCentral Education Cooperative, in south-central South Dakota, are attracting great attention and strongly supported by State Education Secretary Melody Schopp. The project director, Dan Guericke, has established demonstration schools with fewer than 100 students offering curriculum comparable to that of a neighbouring school with 500 or more students. "Size and quality are no longer related," Guericke told the *Argus Leader* in February 2013, "where the teachers are located is irrelevant with the use of technology" (Verges 2013).

Alberta has created the Renewed Funding Framework, similar to Nova Scotia's Small Isolated Schools Supplement, providing rural school boards with additional funds for provincial initiatives that address areas unique to rural communities, such as enrolment decline, small schools by necessity, rural transportation, intra-jurisdictional distance, fuel price contingency, and Hutterite colony schools. This type of funding has great promise for small rural schools, as long as transparent procedures show that this funding supports targeted schools and does not just end up in the school board's general coffers.

We are regularly told that meeting the challenges of the twenty-first century will require Nova Scotians, young and not-so-young, to become more creative, innovative, adaptable citizens capable of thinking strategically and solving our own problems. What better way of developing, honing, and advancing those twenty-first-century skills than to apply them in tackling the most formidable challenge on the Nova Scotian horizon. Starting in February 2013, the Nova Scotia Commission on the New Economy created some forward movement. The time for introspection and public chatter is over and now it's time to get on with closing the yawning urban-rural gap and seriously addressing those glaring social and economic disparities. With this appeal, we call upon the premier and Cabinet, business and education leaders, to put a shoulder to the wheel and get on with alleviating the economic, social, and environmental issues of our time. Start with rural and small town Nova Scotia.

Closing successful small rural schools undermines two, if not three, of the pillars towards achieving a sustainable, thriving community — economic, social, and environmental prosperity.

Access to public education is clearly linked to the social and economic prosperity of rural areas, yet the closure of schools, presented as a way of improving "educational outcomes," fails to recognize the real losses — the loss of the child's sense of community belonging, the impact upon family life, and the further separation of families from their schools.

Toward a Social Sustainability Framework

The Nova Scotia Social Prosperity Framework, *Weaving the Threads*, attempted to chart a way to a better future for all Nova Scotians. Pursuing social prosperity requires a major shift in thinking and priorities in a province facing serious economic challenges and inclined to tackle issues in an incremental, *ad hoc* fashion. While attractive in conception, the framework tended to be diffuse, embracing a broad philosophy supposedly exemplified in some two-dozen existing or new public sector cultural support programs (Nova Scotia Government 2010: 35–40). It was not robust enough for the Dexter NDP Government, with its more immediate "job creation" agenda. Indeed, the Nova Scotia Commission on the New Economy eschewed the Social Prosperity Framework in embracing a more entrepreneurial innovation and "wealth creation" agenda (Nova Scotia Commission on the New Economy 2013).

The following critical element is missing in Nova Scotia's go-forward economic and regional development strategy: a far more creative approach known in the United Kingdom as "social sustainability." It actually found its origins in the U.K. in the late 1990s when Sir John Egan investigated the British construction industry and began undertaking a thorough study of what makes for sustainable communities. In 2003, the U.K. government commissioned Egan to clarify the meaning of "community sustainability" and to identify the necessary skills to create sustainable communities. The Egan Review, published in 2004, found that social sustainability was determined by a few key factors: governance, social and cultural, housing and the built environment, economy, environmental, services and transport, and connectivity (Egan 2004). The Social Prosperity agenda referenced social sustainability as the desire of Nova Scotians for "the same — and hopefully better — quality of life for future generations as we have or want for ourselves" (Nova Scotia Government 2010: 9).

Community building efforts, like the planning and design of new housing subdivisions, are paying much more attention to creating and re-generating socially sustainable communities. In this newly emerging area of social policy and facilities planning, traditional areas and principles, such as equity and health, are converging with a newer focus on participation, needs, social capital, the economy, the environment, and — more recently — with notions of "happiness, well being, and quality of life" (Colantonio and Dixon 2009). A December 2005 report prepared by Joy Elliott for the Coastal Communities Network helped to connect the dots. The future of Nova Scotia's endangered schools and threatened rural communities will, in all likelihood, be determined by the receptivity and willingness of provincial authorities and school boards to embrace that broader outlook rooted in an understanding of what makes for sustainable, thriving communities. Simply put, it's time for Nova Scotia to get its act together, for the sake of the very survival of rural and small town life.

Embracing a Rural World View

System-wide initiatives will do little to promote rural regeneration without significant changes in the Nova Scotia school curriculum and pedagogy. Rural dwellers have their own world view, and they do not see it reflected in the educational priories, organizational framework, or school curriculum produced by the Nova Scotia Department of Education and delivered by regional school boards. Rural community leaders like Kate Oland of Middle River, Steven Rhude of Wolfville, Troy Greencorn of Canso, and Leif Helmer of Petite Riviere simply do not accept the so-called "cities agenda" and consciously reject the notion that dynamism and creativity are the preserve of urban places. By their life choices, they are championing rurality and mounting resistance against the forces of modernity promoting the idea that rural places should be "left to die" (Corbett 2006: 290).

The rural world view not only persists but is experiencing a revival in villages and rural communities far removed from HRM and the central corridor of Nova Scotia. The collapse of the fishery and the fading of resource extraction industries has led to outmigration, but the rural dwellers remaining are still strongly attached to these rural places despite no longer serving their initial economic purpose as outposts for fishing, mining, or pulp and paper-making. Many rural folk, old and recently arrived, tend to see Halifax and even smaller cities like Sydney as "parasitic spaces draining resources

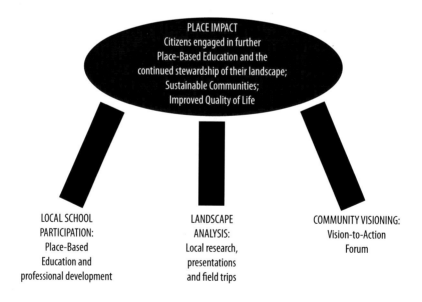

Since the appearance of David Sobel's 2002 book Place-Based Education: Connecting Classroom and Community, the new curriculum philosophy has been championed by New England educators, supported by the University of Vermont.

and people out of the real sites of production, rural communities." To them, rural places are still the backbone of the province's traditional society and economy. Indeed, urban spaces are full of essentially unproductive people who do not perform real work or contribute to society's sustenance. Power blackouts, rain storms, and traffic jams threaten urban dwellers who live in "networked cocoons" and are easily panicked by technocratic system failures (Corbett 2006: 290). Leading voices of rural Nova Scotia, like Troy Greencorn, executive director of Canso's Stan Rogers Folk Festival, see rural dwellers as "the real purveyors of economic change" and express utter disdain for "centralized agencies" like Regional Development Authorities (RDAs) funnelling government monies to regional offices in New Glasgow, Bridgewater, and Antigonish (Greencorn 2012).

Fashioning a Rural, Place-Based Curriculum

Centrally developed and managed school curricula tend to serve the demands and needs of a corporatist, managed, and networked urban society, even in Nova Scotia and elsewhere in the Maritimes. Yet, as Acadia University's Michael Corbett aptly observes, rural places will not go away. "Rustic spaces," he points out, "continue to haunt our global consumer society and our forward-looking modernist education system" (2006: 291). Instead of fading from the scene, they persist and stand in the way of urban modernizers seeking to "develop" rural places as sources of resources and labour to fuel the urban, technocratic, globalized economy. Seeing themselves as essential "stewards of the land," rural dwellers instinctively resist being human fodder or "redundant labour" in a post-industrial society. Surrounded by a world too large to be controlled, rural dwellers seek to "shrink it back to their size and reach" and "anchor themselves in places" where they can "recall their historic memories" (Castells 2004 : 69). Corbett claims that in such a situation, "place-based history, culture, and tradition" assume larger importance and could well form the basis for "a productive, life-sustaining infrastructure" and a local community-based curriculum that speaks to the needs and aspirations of rural children (Corbett 2006: 291–92).

Small rural schools are uniquely positioned to offer essentially free community-based programs and to involve far more children in school activities. Local organizations like the Kinsmen and 4H Club are communitarian agencies that provide access to community resources and a range of voluntary activities. In rural villages and small towns, they often provide services filled by public sector agencies in cities and larger towns. Small school advocates, at every school review meeting, lineup to testify to the superiority of small schools in involving larger numbers of children in school life. This only confirms the following claim, made by Verner Smitheram, a fierce opponent of P.E.I. school consolidation, three decades ago: "Only a small percentage of students in a big school can participate in a play, while almost all can become involved in a production staged by a very small school.... The same applies to sports, clubs, and academics" (1982). What was true thirty years ago is even truer today, especially when one compares levels of school engagement for bused-in students in "big box" elementary schools with that in small rural schools.

Teaching and learning in Nova Scotia schools, rural as well as urban, is now driven, to a surprising degree, by the education accountability agenda. Most of the provincial curricula and guidelines pay homage to the standardized, "one-size-fits-all' program of provincial testing and accountability. In rural regional high schools and even local elementary schools, educators are trained to implement standardized student assessments, outcome-based learning, and data-driven reporting. Child development philosophy, social justice and equity initiatives, and "success for all" programs tend to counterbalance somewhat the full force of system-wide testing and accountability in elementary schools. Nevertheless, system-wide testing in mathematics and literacy cuts into instructional time for supposedly "soft subjects," like social studies and environmental science. All of this erodes the time available for programs that Australian rural educators consider essential to "education for sustainability" (Boon 2011).

Provincial education policy remains essentially blind to the realities of rurality and to the unique interests and needs of Nova Scotia's rural students and teachers. School consolidation is massing larger numbers of rural students in "big box" elementary schools and distant rural high schools which are patterned, in many ways, after standard urban and suburban schools. Rural high schools, in Corbett's words, are "constructed as launching pads for the academically able" rather than being built on a more human scale, offering a place-based curriculum, and responding to local community interests. Although most teachers trained at Acadia University, St. Francis Xavier University, and Cape Breton University end up teaching in rural or small town schools, little is done to prepare them for that experience (Corbett 2006: 294). In spite of the red flags raised in Michael Corbett's *Learning to Leave*, most schools continue to function as if their mission is to educate rural students to "make it" in the outside urban world far from their home communities (Corbett 2008). One of the great advantages of transforming small rural schools into community hubs would be the ability to provide a much more community-rooted, place-based, socially responsible curriculum. With the right approach and in the right hands, community-schools of this type might become crucibles for the fashioning of young rural minds steeped in rural ways and committed to stewardship, ecological sensitivity, local enterprise, and rural revitalization.

6

Community-Building
The Case for Public Engagement

"Parents and community members should be involved earlier in discussions about the future of schools.... Boards should look at groups or families of schools before focusing on individual schools for review." — Nova Scotia Education, *Kids and Learning First* (February 2012) p. 17

"Successful schools are not the result of successful buildings ... it is unacceptable to move and divide our communities." — Gerald Toney, Mi'kmaw Elder, Annapolis Valley First Nation, on the *Successful Schools and Successful Students* Plan, AVRSB School Board Meeting, 6 March, 2012

A school review process is not a sufficient basis for charting the future shape and direction of Nova Scotia's public education system. The priorities driving that process are facilities and space planning and the desire to achieve economies of scale and operational efficiencies. The quality of education, student engagement, and strengthening school-community relations are the fundamental goals of Nova Scotia education, but those goals do not factor in the current planning model embodied in reducing the "overhead" (overgrown structures and administration) and school consolidation.

Nova Scotia's *Kids and Learning First* does open the door to looking at a new approach to restructuring the system. The plan is sprinkled with innovative ideas and demonstrates an inclination to "do things differently" in the twenty-first century: "Parents and community members should be involved earlier in discussions about the future of schools." That is critical to meeting the challenges facing rural education, but it is just a beginning. What we really need is a way of translating those good intentions into public policy and practice.

The approach recommended, albeit by default, falls far short of those aspirations. Indeed, the plan seems to accept the school review process as the sum total of forward planning activities. One key section of *Kids and Learning First* suggests that ensuring fairness in administering the system is all that can be expected in the future. When reviewing schools for possible closure, we are presented with a scrupulously balanced list that includes "appropriate spaces to deliver programs, [including] access to specialist teachers and resources, access to cafeterias, extra-curricular opportunities, travel time for students, the impact of declining enrolments, and age of schools." There is some recognition that schools inhabit communities, but that amounts to a planning sugges-tion that "families of schools" be considered, not just single schools, in rendering closure de-cisions (Nova Scotia Education 2012: 16–17).

When pressed for an ex-emplary school review process, Education Minister Ramona Jennex and senior education officials are quick to cite the *Successful Schools for Successful*

"Bigger isn't better" was the clear message voiced at the Save our Schools Rally held in April 2010 at St. Ninian's Place, Antigonish. (Private collection)

Students planning process implemented by the Annapolis Valley Regional School Board, initiated in September 2008 and extending until the end of the 2012–13 school year. It is touted as a model exemplifying strategic facilities planning, community consultation, and school-community collaboration. It does reflect modern school planning design principles, allows for community input, and is carried out *before* embarking on the legislated provincial school review process. When the Nova Scotia Small Schools Initiative delegation presented its brief to the minister on May 15, 2012, she asked if the present-ers had seen the AVRSB model and suggested that it was working well to build bridges and still allow for the achievement of board objectives. Nova Scotia's opposition leader, Stephen McNeil, the MLA for Annapolis, told the Liberal Party Convention in March 2012 that he too saw nothing wrong with the smooth, staged school review process in his region.

The Preferred Model — Under the Microscope

In contrast, school communities governed by the Annapolis Valley Regional Board, such as Newport Station, Cambridge, and even Annapolis Royal, are not enamoured at all by that board's school review process because, in each case, it zeroed-in on their local school, targeting it for closure. A closer look at how the process rolled out and its net impact on rural school communities is revealing as it renders visible the AVRSB's real school facilities planning priorities, its "hidden agenda," mode of operations, and bottom-line objectives (AVRSB 2011).

The five core objectives of the AVRSB's Successful Schools for Successful Students model (2008–2010) are those of the facilities planner wedded to traditional school planning assumptions and doctrinal beliefs. The starting point for the school board was facilities, facilities, facilities, and specifically, "the conditions of school buildings, facility operating costs and enrolment trends, both past and future." Enrolment declines were clearly driving the whole process. It was noted back in 2008, for example, that from board amalgamation in 1996 until September 2007 the board had lost more than 2,910 students (16 percent) but was "operating considerably more school square footage." Over the next two years, the board reported losing 535 more students and identified areas, mostly rural, where the declines were greater (AVRSB 2010: 1). The AVRSB's single focus, right from the beginning, was to reduce its footprint and to rely upon consolidation as the tried, tested, and only acceptable means of offloading underutilized space in the system.

The Program Delivery Model, first proposed in 2009 by Dr. Jim Gunn and known as "grade reconfiguration," accepted as gospel and enshrined as "the preferred grade configuration" for program delivery of Primary to Grade 5 for elementary, Grades 6 to 8 for middle school, and Grades 9 to 12 for high school. It was, the board claimed, not Gunn's at all, but rather the formula generated out of the first round of "public consultations" in 2008–09. It became a sort of template that pre-determined the outcomes of any subsequent school-community consultations. The official rationale was to ensure that the numbers of transitions experienced by students was minimized as much as possible. The rollout from 2008 until 2012 went like this: first came the "grade configuration template," then the identification reports, and finally the review for closure process, conducted in two waves. The overriding goal, the AVRSB kept insisting, was "not primarily directed to reducing the number of schools in the region, but rather to rationalize the way the educational program would be delivered into the future" (AVRSB 2010: 2).

The parameters set for the whole protracted AVRSB school facilities planning and review exercise put facilities ahead of students, families, and communities. It was driven by these five objectives: to implement the board's "preferred grade configuration," to determine "the future need for and use of school facilities," to "review current school catchments areas," to "identify facilities requiring major capital improvements or replacement, " and to examine "school schedules to determine if changes are warranted" in the daily and weekly program. (Kelly, *The Register*, February 2, 2012). All five of the stated objectives speak to facilities matters and make no reference to improving the quality of education, ensuring healthy, sustainable schools, or building thriving school communities.

The AVRSB school review process eventually claimed only two schools, the historic Annapolis Royal Regional Academy, serving Grades 6 to 8, and Newport Station District School, serving Primary to Grade 6 (AVRSB, School Reviews, 2013). That was, however, just the most visible manifestation of the "rationalization" of school organization and program delivery across the whole school district. A few threatened schools survived the axe, including Cambridge School in Kings County as well as Three Mile Plains School and Windsor Forks School in West Hants. In each case, they were granted reprieves until the next time or until the province coughs up the funding for a promised super-sized school a bus ride away.

The threat to Cambridge School was beaten back by a vocal, organized, and effective resistance movement. A community school committee, spearheaded by Trish Rafuse, charged that Cambridge School was "the forgotten school," neglected by the AVRSB while "all kinds of renovation and new construction at schools" happened all around the village (Kelly 2011). In January 2012, Rafuse and her parent group demanded to know the answer to a simple question: "Exactly why can't the school be renovated?" At the public meeting, parents rose in unison calling for the school to remain a Primary–8 school (Kelly 2012a). In the case of Cambridge School, the Annapolis Valley First Nation played a critical role in blocking the board's clumsily worded proposal "not to include this building in future planning." Mi'kmaw elder Gerald Toney cut to the chase in rejecting the scheme. "Successful schools are not the result of successful buildings," he declared at the public hearing, adding, "it is unacceptable to move and divide our communities" (Kelly 2012b). Faced with combined Mi'kmaq and parent opposition, Tait and the school board relented, sparing that school.

The fight to save Newport Station District School was a classic school closure battle, much like those waged in village after village in rural Nova Scotia. The P–6 school erected in 1963 enrolled eighty-two students in 2010–11, but it was rated as very well-maintained and located on the eastern fringes of the school board region, bordering the Halifax population growth corridor. The Identification Report issued by the AVRSB in February 2011 was only twelve pages long, including data tables cribbed from official statistical sources and electronically pasted into the document. In the board's own reports, Grade 6 was assumed to be moving out to conform with the

Steven Rhude and Paul Bennett stand in front of abandoned Yarmouth schools on the Nova Scotia school board tour to promote more democratic public engagement. (Tina Comeau, The Vanguard)

new grade reconfiguration scheme, and no real claim was made that closure would save much money for taxpayers, factoring in the loss of a provincial small schools grant.

The Newport Station School Study Committee report, entitled *In Pursuit of Educational Excellence*, prepared in January 2012 by Debbie Francis and ten other volunteer parents, presented a mountain of evidence in support of keeping the school open. That 185-page report, including a Save Our School Petition with more than 500 signatures, made a compelling and passionate case for retaining the school, given its quality of program, community support, and close proximity to proposed new subdivisions. The NSDS parents won the public debate by "a country mile, "but still lost their school" (Delaney 2012). A year later, in January 2013, Superintendent Tait was at it again, this time promoting a One Big School solution for Newport Station students and two neighbouring schools, Three Mile Plains and Windsor Forks District School (Kelley, WFDS Home & School Letters, 2013). In this relentless consolidation process, you lose your school, tune-out, and wake-up to discover a new proposal to bus your kids to a 350 student "Big Box elementary" down the country road.

What are the lessons to be learned from dissecting the AVRSB model? The board's school planning process is a polished, professionally packaged process shepherding identified schools on a well-marked road leading to "grade reconfiguration" and more school consolidation. It is only lauded by Superintendent Margo Tait and its defenders because it succeeded in moving forward the provincial school reorganization agenda and in securing the closure of small schools and ultimately their consolidation into "super-sized" schools. Creating the illusion of public participation in the process was what helped to override and ultimately squash any dissent in the communities put through the wringer not once, but twice, over four years.

Call for a More Democratic and Legitimate Process

What Nova Scotia needs is a whole new approach to rural revitalization, encompassing and supplanting the current school review for closure system. Announcing the 2013 moratorium on school reviews has bought some breathing space, but should now be utilized as a chance to reinvent the system. Now that Nova Scotia has made that move, public engagement has become the priority as Nova Scotians come together to confront the future and join in a project aimed at finding much more satisfactory community-based decisions. Some rural schools may close, but at least it will be the ones that have failed to secure sufficient community support to remain viable.

The future of Nova Scotia public education lies in restoring public confidence and in promoting system-wide reform through genuine public engagement. During the period of the moratorium, the Department of Education, school boards, regional development agencies, municipal councils, citizens, school councils, and teachers will be challenged to develop an integrated rural education and development strategy and to come up with a public engagement model to guide future planning. The model of public engagement espoused by the Ottawa-based Public Policy Forum might well serve as the lead process in a new policy development framework where the school review process remains only as a last resort to resolve an impasse in community-based decision-making.

The Public Policy Forum's model of public engagement starts by taking a broader lens and breaking out of the old mould that *constrained public policy-making within the educational system.* The new approach should meet two fundamental test questions to achieve legitimacy: First, are we asking the right question — and are we allowing participants to re-frame the fundamental question? And secondly, what are the participants prepared to do, working in partnership with government authorities, to demonstrate ownership of the community-based solutions? Public engagement, Don Lenihan points out, "treats issues holistically from the start. It allows participants to propose new connections between issues and to explain why these links are important. By giving participants a chance to get this on the table, the engagement approach ensures that everyone feels included and reassures them that … the reframing [of] the question — will not be swept under the rug" (Lenihan 2012: 120).

A public engagement process that is narrowly defined and superficial will secure lip service support from volunteer enthusiasts or be dismissed outright by reformers as another window dressing exercise. Breaking the traditional formal consultation mould will require the Department and ultimately local school boards to embrace a completely new framework and set of principles.

"SCHOOL SAVED - COMMUNITY LIVES"

A victory photo taken by Larry Donald Haight and posted on the Save Weymouth Consolidated School Facebook page, March 2012.

The Nova Scotia Department of Education should take the lead in developing a public engagement model for rural education and development with two fundamental goals:

- to save viable small schools from closure and rural communities from extinction; and
- to transform the school review process into a community-building initiative rather than an energy-sapping, frustrating, and frequently disillusioning process.

Such a model would be based upon the following assumptions:

- schools are social anchors and economic drivers at the centre of local communities;
- small communities are threatened in rural and small town Nova Scotia and we need to develop a broad rural revitalization strategy;
- the existing school review process is adversarial, seriously flawed, and too often divisive;
- it is important to find community-initiated and community-based solutions; and
- technology can bridge distances and "networked schools" have great potential.

The public engagement model unveiled by the Public Policy Forum in January 2012 is a sound, research-based model designed to meet the new realities facing twenty-first-century governments. The model provides a viable means to achieving community-based, broadly accepted public policy decisions.

The key principles of the Public Policy Forum's model (Lenihan 2012: 122–28) respond to changing societal dynamics and best practice in other fields. Following are eighteen important principles, in point form:

1. Recognize and respond to the new public policy environment — finding solutions now requires participation of *all the players.*
2. New public expectations are clear — to be more transparent, accountable, and responsive.
3. Good policy is comprehensive — recognizes interdependence of fields (more holistic).
4. A new set of goals is emerging — balancing sustainability, wellness, lifelong learning with purely financial goals.
5. Real progress toward societal goals requires public participation — breaking the mould.
6. Taking responsibility implies having some control — give the community a much greater say in the process.
7. The best decisions are made collaboratively — it's about collaboration, not devolution.
8. Accountability is shared — joint decisions win broader public support.
9. Securing and sustaining trust — success requires trust but also builds trust.
10. Public engagement is inclusive — bring everyone to the table.
11. Every community is different — treat every situation as unique, avoid systems.
12. Local governments are the gateway to the public — best solutions are local.
13. Citizen's voices must be heard — giving citizens a meaningful voice is critical to success.
14. Public engagement is scalable — success in one local community breeds success elsewhere.
15. Policy and service delivery are linked — link policy to practice (i.e, shared services).
16. Collaboration requires a new measurement framework — establish benchmarks for trust, openness, inclusiveness, mutual respect, personal responsibility.
17. Sustaining change requires ongoing dialogue and action — it's not static but dynamic.
18. True public engagement breeds ownership of the decisions, changes the whole political dynamic, and builds support for institutions, programs, and services.

School reviews pit school boards against public school parents and divide communities. Although the Annapolis Valley Regional Board developed a more protracted, ongoing school facilities planning process that purports to provide parents and citizens with formal opportunities for public input and representations, its model (2008–2012) does not stand up to close scrutiny

SAVE OUR SCHOOL
Public Hearing on Thursday February 21st

The School Board will be at our school to hear from residents,
parents, students, graduates etc
February 21st at 6:30pm
Petite Riviere Elementary School
123 Wentzell Road

You can speak, read a statement, or write in to provide input.
Call the board office for more info 541-3000 or to obtain
a copy of the Review documents.

A widely distributed notice prepared by Leif Helmer to rally the village of Petite Riviere in support of their small community school.

and falls short of being true public engagement in some vitally important ways. Its core philosophy favours building management priorities over community-building activities aimed at finding joint and mutually agreeable solutions. Adopting a system-wide "grade configuration" template and then managing consultations in such a way as to advance that scheme strongly suggests that "the ends justify the means" in the Annapolis Valley system. There is, as school reformers well know, no substitute for real public engagement. Genuine public engagement would also be far more likely to produce community-based, longer-term solutions to the problems besetting rural and small town Nova Scotia.

Significant changes are afoot in many Canadian public bodies, private businesses, and community organizations that seek to build public support for major initiatives by involving the public in more meaningful ways in the making of a wider range of decisions. The Halifax Public Libraries was one of the first organizations in the Atlantic Region to embrace the new philosophy of public engagement. It did so in conducting its public consultations in the spring and summer of 2011 over the design and internal layout of its $55 million Central Library on Spring Garden Road in downtown Halifax. The main architect of the library public engagement project was Tim Merry, co-founder of the Art of Hosting movement. "With the library," Merry told *Progress Magazine*, "we saw the potential to do something that was more than just participatory events, so we asked how could we include street engagement plus interactive platforms?" Live Library consultations utilized the World Café discussion group format, fully evolved with live streaming, targeted focus groups, surveys, and a "mind map" graffiti wall.

The community-led consultations won over initial doubters like Danish design architect Morten Schmidt, who worked with Halifax's Fowler Bauld & Mitchell on the project. "For the first time in my career," Schmidt said, "the public truly became my client" (Haynes 2013: 43). The Central Library consultations proved so successful that developer Joe Ramia adopted the model in the second round of public consultation over the controversial Nova Convention Centre, and groups in Alberta, Pictou County, and Washington, D.C. are utilizing similar public engagement strategies.

Provincial education authorities have been slow to embrace the new philosophy of public engagement. In spite of the spread of the EdCamp movement across the United States and into Western Canada, the Nova Scotia Government and school boards continue to conduct public consultations in traditional "teacher knows best" mode, laying out "hard proposals" and then soliciting responses. True public engagement cannot, and will not, result from such top-down approaches, especially with today's skeptical public. "For multiple reasons — information saturation, social uncertainty, and the nature of technology," Merry claims, "we're seeing a paradigm shift from command and control to participatory leadership." The primary lesson to be learned, according to Merry, may be this: "The age of the individual expert is over; now it is more about everybody bringing their experience to find solutions none of us could create alone" (Haynes 2013: 44). That is very much in evidence when you survey the comprehensive School Study Committee reports generated by groups of volunteers in communities like Middle River, Heatherton, Petite Riviere, and Newport Station in the last two rounds of school reviews. For Nova Scotia's Education Department and regional school boards, that message has yet to sink in. When it does, the school review process will be put permanently on ice.

7

The Response
Mushrooming Popular Support and Official Silence

"To meet that demographic challenge, the province needs to develop a new model for small community schooling, just as it has done for primary health care with community collaborative-care centres. More virtual schooling should play a part. But a broader vision of the local school is needed, too, as a new province-wide reform group, the Small Schools Delegation, is advocating in its lively Nova Scotia Small Schools Initiative, on Facebook." — Editorial, "New Model Schooling: The Heart of a Revival," *Chronicle Herald*, May 27, 2012

"I acknowledge receipt of your unsolicited brief *Schools at the Centre: A Revitalization Strategy for Rural Communities* which I will be reviewing with my staff." — Hon. Ramona Jennex, Minister of Education, Letter of reply, May 31, 2012

The *Schools at the Centre* report (NSSSI 2012), presented to Education Minister Ramona Jennex on May 15, 2012, created quite a public stir, particularly in rural and small town Nova Scotia. A news story in the *Chronicle Herald* two days later gave full coverage to the Nova Scotia Small Schools Delegation brief and meeting with the minister. The core message that rural schools should be seen as "the centre of their communities" and "a key part of economic development" got out, as did the group's call to "push the reset button and take a completely different approach" to the school review for closure process. Stopping the school review process for a year to give the province time to develop "an integrated approach to rural revitalization that includes local schools" was received as a common sense approach to future development. Parent activist Kate Oland of Middle River, Victoria County, put the whole issue in a larger context: "Stop looking at education as separate from health, as separate from economic development, as separate from tourism. They're all linked in a rural landscape. All of those things must work together" (Shiers 2012).

Education Minister Jennex and Deputy Minister Rosalind Penfound listened intently to the May 15, 2012, brief presentation in the minister's board room, closely watching the clock. The call for a province-wide moratorium on school closures caught them completely off guard and so did the direct appeal for the minister to intervene to stop the rural carnage. One after another, members of the delegation made impassioned pleas for the minister to take the lead in halting the rural school closures, promoting an integrated rural strategy, and adopting a more open public engagement process to find community-based solutions. After listening politely, the minister responded with only two questions. First, she asked "How widespread is bullying on the long bus rides?" Then, she mentioned the Annapolis Valley Regional School Board's school planning process, and asked what the delegation thought of that approach. It was abundantly clear that she favoured the protracted, traditional school review process. When pressed for a response, she requested more time to consider the brief and made no real commitment one way or the other.

The delegation got its answer in a news report in the South Shore weekly paper later that week. Minister Jennex flatly rejected the Small Schools Initiative's appeal for a cessation in the school review process. On May 19, the *Chronicle Herald* ran a full column, signed by eight members of the delegation, re-stating the call for a moratorium on school closures and calling for a "community-based, rural economic and social development" strategy to give Nova Scotia's rural communities "some reason for hope in the 21st century (Bennett et al. 2012). One week to the day after the initial presentation, Paul W. Bennett, Kate Oland, Michelle Wamboldt, Barry Olivella, and Ron Stockton presented the report to Paul Black, Director of Community Relations, and David Mackenzie, Social Policy Advisor, in the Office of the Premier, at One Government Place. That presentation stressed the delegation's desire to work *with, not against,* the government to come to the rescue of rural schools and communities. The timing was good, Black advised us, coming on the heels of the federal government's decision to cut funding to Nova Scotia's Rural Development Authorities.

It turned out to be the last the delegation ever heard from anyone in the Nova Scotia NDP government, until the end of that month. On May 31, 2012, Paul W. Bennett received a four line letter from the minister of education, which read as follows: "I write in follow-up to our meeting on Tuesday May 15, 2012, at which time you were accompanied by several other individuals. I acknowledge receipt of your unsolicited brief *Schools at the Centre: A Revitalization Strategy for Rural Communities* which I will be reviewing with my staff. Sincerely, Ramona Jennex, Minister of Education." That was it, the only response ever received from the minister or her Department.

The Small Schools Delegation was undeterred by the cool official reception. Shortly after the official presentation to the minister, the Delegation established its online presence as the Nova Scotia Small Schools Initiative on Facebook. With Kate Oland and Paul W. Bennett acting as co-curators of the site, the Initiative attracted not only attention but 250 dedicated followers within its first two weeks. The vast majority of the initial wave of followers were veterans of school closure battles or parents with schools identified for possible shutdown in the next cycle of closures. That Facebook site quickly became the "populist" nerve centre and clearing house for reports on school closures and all types of threats to the future of rural and small town Nova Scotia. It was also, judging from the online actions of the minister and her officials, a convenient way of keeping track of the pesky small school activists abroad in the province.

The Small School Initiative supporters were buoyed by the strong and consistent support of the Halifax *Chronicle Herald* and its editorial board. On May 27, 2012, the *Herald* ran an editorial essentially endorsing the *Schools at the Centre* vision and plan for revitalizing rural communities. Embracing the Initiative's call for a "New Model of Schooling" for rural Nova Scotia, the paper added its voice to the Small Schools campaign:

> To meet that demographic challenge, the province needs to develop a new model for small community schooling, just as it has done for primary health care with community collaborative-care centres. More virtual schooling should play a part. But a broader vision of the local school is needed, too, as a new province-wide reform group, the Small Schools Delegation, is advocating in its lively Nova Scotia Small Schools Initiative, on Facebook.
>
> In a brief to Education Minister Ramona Jennex, the group wants the province to make efficient, small schools the heart of a rural revitalization strategy. It's asking the government to suspend school closures while devising this plan and to work with communities to turn schools into multi-service assets.
>
> Premier Darrell Dexter should take up this invitation. He himself espoused very similar ideas in 2006 when he called for a two-year moratorium on school closures, a broad review of the role of schools in community development, and an examination of new services that could be delivered at school sites.
>
> Back then, Mr. Dexter lamented that removing a school from a small community "is like pulling threads from a blanket." The community fabric gets thinner, a venue for many services disappears, young families are less willing to live there.
>
> The premier now has a chance to stop the unravelling. He should make effective new models of community schooling a priority, as he's already done for community health care. (*Chronicle Herald* 2012b)

Critical support from the province's widely read newspaper has given the movement wings and helped it grow in credibility and strength from May 2012 until March of 2013.

Origins of the Small Schools Initiative

The Nova small schools movement was not an overnight sensation but rather the result of a gathering of small school forces, emerging out of a succession of school closure battles. Its initial catalyst was the divisive and volatile school review process of 2009–10 in Nova Scotia's Strait Regional School Board (SRSB). That bitterly contested battle, centred mainly in Antigonish County, pitted spirited local parents against former Superintendent Jack Beaton and his compliant elected school board. In March 2010, the Strait Regional School Board, based in Port Hastings, voted to close one of its schools, St. Mary's Education Centre elementary school in Sherbrooke, and announced plans to move forward with reviews of three more schools. Superintendent Beaton made the case that the board was reviewing schools for financial reasons. He stated that, over the previous decade, the Strait board had lost 1,000 students while maintaining the same square footage of classroom space that it had in 2000. The St. Mary's Education Centre decision was presented as an amalgamation rather than an outright closure.

The St. Mary's school amalgamation triggered quite a reaction. Moving forward with the next three school accommodation reviews promised to be a rocky road. On March 21, 2010, a full-blown Save Community Schools group was formed, composed of active parents representing all three schools: Rev. H.J. MacDonald elementary (P–6) school, in Heatherton, Antigonish Co., H.M. MacDonald elementary (P–6) school, in Maryvale, Antigonish Co., and Canso Academy high school (9–12), in Canso, Guysborough County. By early April, the coalition had its own website and was fully engaged in whipping up a storm of protest. Two local school trustees, Frank Machnik and Richelle MacLaughlin, broke ranks and sought to exempt the Heatherton and Maryvale schools from the review process. Small schools advocate Dr. Michael Corbett of Acadia University's School of Education was invited to address a major public meeting on April 23, 2010, at St. Ninian's Place, Antigonish, which served as a rallying point for the coalition forces. In addition, his research report, co-authored with Dennis Mulcahy, was posted online and made accessible to all members of the growing coalition of parents. Throughout 2010 and 2011, SaveCommunitySchools.ca, led by two very determined and effective parent activists, Denise Delorey and Randy Delorey of Heatherton, kept the fledgling movement alive (Bennett 2011: 162–64).

A second wave of small school activists emerged on Nova Scotia's South Shore, driven by mounting resistance to school closures in March 2011 and sparked by the minister of education's firing, in late November 2011, of the entire elected South Shore Regional School Board (SSRSB). The dismissal was precipitated when the elected board unexpectedly halted its school review process, throwing Superintendent Nancy Pinch-Worthylake and the senior administration into panic. Pressured from all sides, the elected board, under Chair Elliott Payzant, dissolved into warring factions and eventually resorted to calling for a governance review. That resulted in the firing of the entire elected board and the installation of retired bureaucrat, Judith Sullivan-Corney of Dartmouth, as a one-person board until elections, expected in October 2012 (Ware 2011). No sooner had Sullivan-Corney arrived than the school review process resumed, this time identifying five more schools for possible closure.

With four schools in Lunenburg County already lying abandoned, including the historic Lunenburg Academy, local residents girded themselves for another round of school closure skirmishes. A young parent, Michelle Wamboldt, stepped forward when she got wind that her local school, Petite Riviere Elementary School, was next on the block, along with Pentz Elementary School, in the same school district. Wamboldt found an ally in Christopher Gill, a retired federal civil servant and local artist, living in her village. Without knowing anything much about the Antigonish-based Save Community Schools group, she joined up with fellow Petite Riviere resident Leif Helmer, a popular teacher at NSCC Bridgewater. Together, they planned the Small Schools Summit, held January 21, 2012, on the NSCC Bridgewater Campus. The featured speaker, once again, was Dr. Michael Corbett, and some fifty-five curious delegates showed-up for the Saturday afternoon workshop (Lindsay 2012). It was a genuine populist effort, organized by Helmer and Wamboldt on their own. The summit attracted a real mix of participants, including Sullivan-Corney, Vanda Dow, President of the Nova Scotia Home and School Association, and Michael Bowen, a professor of education at Mount Saint Vincent University. It ended up being a consciousness-raising workshop, and the founders of Save Community Schools, Randy and Denise Delorey, completely immersed in the fight to save their threatened Heatherton School, were not even in attendance.

The Small School Summit proved to be an important catalyst for an emerging province-wide movement. As the summit broke up, a fundamental question was being asked — what comes next? Two founders of Students First Nova Scotia, Paul W. Bennett and Lunenburg lawyer Ron Stockton, approached Wamboldt about formulating a policy brief, mounting a small schools delegation, and taking the message directly to the minister of education. Wamboldt was receptive, and soon a core group began to emerge, consisting of Bennett, Wamboldt, Ron Stockton, Lunenburger Barry Olivella, Wolfville painter Steven Rhude, and Small School Summit presenter Sandra Labor, of Shatford Memorial School in Hubbards. Spotting a spirited critique

A poster distributed by Jens Laursen and the Riverport School Study Committee in their ultimately futile struggle to halt the closure of the school so vital to their community's survival. (Poster by Jens Laursen)

of the school review process in the *Chronicle Herald* (Oland 2012), Bennett approached Kate Oland, of Middle River, to join the proposed delegation. Soon after the idea was broached, Randy Delorey joined the group, pledging the full support of the Strait Region's Save Community Schools. The then manager of HB Studios in Bridgewater, Alastair Jarvis, also joined the group, adding considerable innovative spark and wattage. With Weymouth Consolidated School threatened with closure, Larry Donald Haight, of the Weymouth Board of Trade, came on board to represent Southwest Nova Scotia. The delegation was not only taking shape but aggregating some very talented and totally committed volunteer supporters.

On March 7, 2012, Bennett wrote to Education Minister Jennex advising her that a group was being formed to develop a rural education strategy and requesting an opportunity to present a brief to the minister and Department. The minister was given a clear indication that a delegation was taking shape and that the goal was to come up with an alternative to the school review for closure process. "If you would agree to meet with me and the Small Schools group," he emailed, "I can assure you that the focus will be on recommending specific changes that may well keep 'good schools' with incredibly strong community (support) from being shuttered and to avoid leaving a residue of bitterness in the community." Two weeks later, Jennex replied, agreeing to a meeting but proposing that it be held after the end of the legislative session, in May 2012. Over the next six weeks, Bennett and the Small Schools Initiative Research Group met in Halifax and in Lunenburg, held a teleconference, and assembled a forty-two-page brief. The brief, *Schools at the Centre*, was assembled by Bennett and the team over a period of six weeks on an entirely voluntary basis. It was not, as the minister later suggested in an intercepted email, a surprise or an ambush of any kind. At every stage of the brief's development, she was advised of its progress and even given a copy of the document in advance of the meeting.

Populist movements, like the Nova Scotia Small Schools Initiative, the education minister learned, cannot always be channelled, managed, or marginalized. Since the presentation of the brief in May 2012, the NSSSI grew by leaps and bounds, drawing in new groups of supporters and attracting a regular following of 380 on Facebook, with many posts attracting 3,400 or more hits a week. The *Chronicle Herald* continued to support the NSSSI's vision of "a new model of schooling" and to publish news reports from its regional bureaus that were very sympathetic to supporters of small rural schools. Co-founder Kate Oland emerged as a tremendously effective voice for small school advocates, especially in her stirring addresses on the threat to Cape Breton's rural schools and the rural way of life. South Shore artist Chris Gill specialized in producing whimsical coloured sketches and priceless letters to the editor of the *Lunenburg-Bridgewater Bulletin* in his peculiar guise as a government bureaucrat looking down his nose at "quaint rural folk" (Gill 2012b). After halting the closure of Weymouth Consolidated School in March 2012, Larry Donald Haight refused to disappear, lending his support and giving advice to schools in the Southwest region in the sightlines of the Tri-County Regional School Board. In spite of the intense four-year struggle to save the Heatherton school, Randy Delorey continued to provide advice and counsel to small school groups across the provinces, sharing his expertise on the intricacies of *Education Act* requirements and regulations.

The titanic struggle to save H.J. MacDonald Elementary School provided some bitter lessons for Nova Scotia small school advocates. After confronting virtually the entire village of Heatherton at a public hearing in February 2012, the Strait Regional School Board voted 7–4 on March 5, 2012, to close the school. Some 200 public school supporters erupted in outrage when the final vote was tallied in that same gymnasium, but it was all to no avail. The Strait Board, headed by Superintendent Beaton (until his retire-

Chair of the Rev. H.J. MacDonald School Study Committee, Denise Delorey, confronts Superintendent Jack Beaton and Chair Mary Jess MacDonald at the critical public hearing determining the fate of her school. (Private collection)

ment in June 2012), would have its way. The remaining seventy-five students from Primary to Grade 6 were unceremoniously uprooted and sent to other schools in September 2012 (Beswick 2012a). The SRSB claimed that it would save $175,000 to $186,000 by closing the school, but somehow miraculously found $2 million or more in capital funds to renovate the receiving school.

The Deloreys of Heatherton are not the quitting kind. Two months after the board vote, parents Denise Delorey and Jamie Samson launched a law suit against the Strait Regional School Board to keep Rev. H.J. MacDonald open and prevent the public system from abandoning yet another rural Nova Scotia village. Acting on behalf of the Heatherton villagers, they went forward with the first legal challenge of a board's decision to close a school since Nova Scotia adopted its revised school review legislation in 2008. The chair of the SRSB, Mary Jess MacDonald, a veteran school trustee, sounded a rather plaintive cry for help. "I'll take a lot of lumps for the good of students," she told the *Chronicle Herald*, "but this process pits boards and the communities against each other" (Beswick 2012b).

Closing day at Rev. H.J. MacDonald on June 22, 2012, was bittersweet. Local Home and School Association president Denise Delorey took the high road, concealing her deep disillusionment with the whole closure process. "It's been a stressful year," she said, "so today is a fun day to celebrate and tell the students that we appreciate all they've been through." Principal Dave Bance captured well the mood; "We may lose the school but we won't go out with our tail between our legs," he said. "This is a close community with very special children" (Beswick 2012c).

On January 4, 2013, a full six months after the school actually closed, Justice Patrick J. Murray of the Supreme Court of Nova Scotia delivered the final blow. His forty-four-page ruling arrived with a thud and dismissed the suit. His decision makes for depressing reading because it applies a narrow, legally constrained test in assessing the impact of school closures upon students. Trying to prove "irreparable harm" and assessing "balance of convenience" were the criteria applied, based upon previous legal precedents (Supreme Court of Nova Scotia 2012). Proving that busing students to another school causes "irreparable harm" is next to impossible, and, more significantly, the courts give no weight whatsoever to claims that closing a small school does "irreparable harm" to rural communities. The legal route was now exhausted — it was now up to the politicians to set it right.

8

Pathway to Rural Regeneration
Transforming Small Schools
into Community Hubs

"Schools are vital to rural communities. The money that might be saved through consolidation could be forfeited in lost taxes, declining property values, and lost businesses … in communities where the citizenry is civically engaged, local businesses proper, and … these factors anchor populations to place." — Thomas A. Lyson, "What Does a School Mean to a Community?" *Journal of Research in Rural Education* (Winter 2002)

"Good relationships between residents, and a range of local activities — formal and informal –are the key to thriving communities.… Social capital — the quality of relationships between residents that give the community the capability to be supportive and empowered and a rich cultural life — is important for people to put down roots, feel 'secure,' and 'at home' and develop a sense of belonging." — Saffron Woodcraft, *Design for Social Sustainability*, The Young Foundation, 2012, p. 31–32

School closure battles continue to rage each school year, repeating the same destructive school review process, year after year. Throughout 2012–13, three Nova Scotia school boards, Chignecto-Central Regional School Board, South Shore Regional School Board, and Tri-County Regional School Board, put some fourteen local communities through another endurance test. Small villages like Petite Riviere, Maitland, River John, Wentworth, and Mill Village were thrown into crisis, forcing hundreds of rural and small town Nova Scotians to rally in defence of both their elementary schools and their communities (Bennett 2013a). Rural regeneration can — and should — begin in Nova Scotia's villages and small towns, and there is enormous potential to be unlocked in the regions outside of a ninety-minute drive of Halifax. Fully 45 percent of Nova Scotia's population lives in places of less than 5,000 in population, and that is what makes this province truly unique. Rebuilding the faltering rural economy should start rather than end with the schools, providing children and families with a more secure future.

Amidst the upheaval precipitated by school reviews for closure, something was beginning to stir in rural and small town Nova Scotia. Isolated schools in rural communities like Bass River on the Fundy Shore had essentially given up the fight after barely surviving a gruelling 2010 school closure process (Bennett 2011: 148–49). In spite of such setbacks, community resilience began to emerge from the bottom- up, as grassroots community groups, one after another, are rejecting the provincial closure agenda and embracing a "third option" — transforming their under-utilized small schools into "community hubs," building around an "anchor tenant" — the P–6 population of students and teachers. Instead of accepting the law of demographic gravity, they are organizing to re-build their communities and looking to the school boards to join in that project.

The Small Schools Initiative campaign found some unlikely champions. Halifax *Chronicle Herald* columnist Dan Leger jumped into the fray on February 4, 2013, with a persuasive message: To save small communities, start by saving their schools (Leger 2013). Provincial business groups, like the Nova Scotia Chamber of Commerce, based in Truro, and municipal leaders like Don Downe began to speak out publicly in favour of a totally different approach to abandoning schools and downloading the properties on local municipalities. The Union of Nova Scotia Municipalities issued a demographic outlook report in October 2012 that called for action to staunch the hemmorage of people from rural communities outside of Halifax and the so-called central corridor of the province (Canmac Economics 2012). Provincial opinion leaders like Yarmouth journalist Ralph Surette began in the winter of 2012–13 to question the Darrell Dexter government's short-term "job creation" strategy (Surette 2012). While the NDP government tends to view economic development through a narrow lens, the Nova Scotia Small Schools Initiative and many rural Nova Scotians are clamouring for more "out of the box" strategically sound economic and social thinking. The clear message, delivered at public hearings, at kitchen tables, and in general stores, is that plugging the rural population drain should be a much higher priority for the Nova Scotia NDP government.

Looking around outside of HRM and the central corridor, the realities are stark and almost impossible to ignore. School closures in small villages like Riverport, Heatherton, and Newport Station are leaving a bitter harvest of For Sale signs on front lawns and in the remaining shop windows. Big questions call for straight answers: Without rural schools, where will the children and families come from to regenerate the declining rural economy? Without schools, how long do communities survive? Impact assessment reports, following the Department of Education formula, direct school committees to choose

The abandoned Riverport school, boarded up and deteriorating in February 2013, two years after its closure, and now a charge on the taxpayers of Lunenburg County. (Photo: Jens Laursen)

between two losing propositions — the status quo or further consolidation. In a few cases, the second option is worse, splitting up school families and busing these children to scattered sites over poor country roads.

The Emerging Third Option — Community Hub Schools

The seeds of rural regeneration were beginning to sprout in the winter of 2012–13, even in the shadow of the provincially mandated school review process. Study Committees at Petite Riviere, Maitland, and River John rejected the "status quo trap," declined to play the losing game, and generated their own community-based third options. Not content to seek a reprieve, they got busy and produced incredibly innovative, community-building activities to fill the empty spaces and ensure the long-term sustainability of their schools.

What was this new species known as a "community hub school?" "A community hub," according to leading advocate Dr. David Clandfield, is "a central gathering place for people, their activities, and events." It's more than just "a high-use multipurpose centre" and more of "a two-way hub," where "children's learning activities within the school contribute to community development" and, in turn, " community activities contribute to, and enrich, children's learning within the school" (Clandfield 2010: 20).

The community hub model gained considerable traction in 2010 with the appearance of Clandfield's groundbreaking educational policy paper, "The School as Community Hub," published in the Canadian Centre for Policy Alternatives journal *Our School Our Selves*. Clandfield offers a trenchant and deadly accurate critique of the Humberwood Centre, an ultra modern Toronto region "shopping mall high school," which he likened to "a miniature BCE Place" or some sort of "commercial exchange, retail activity, corporate headquarters." He saw that school as an alarming example of the "neo-liberal agenda" invading and undermining the publicly funded school system. Instead of schools as simply a "space for compulsory school attendance," he envisioned a great potential for developing them into "community hubs," or genuine community-based centres of local programming and services.

Nevertheless, Clandfield sees in the promising community hub model a possible threat, looming like a cloud with a dark lining. The challenge, according to Clandfield, is to prevent such "community hub schools" from being appropriated for "neo-liberal" purposes: "privatization, commodification of services, and the conversion of learning for full citizenship into preparation for a world of prosperity-seeking competitiveness where the entrepreneurial few reap benefits at the expense of the regulated many." It is up to school reformers to determine whether the community hub school becomes a vital educational tool for fostering "co-operative community development" or just another manifestation of "an efficient channel" through which to "deliver viable human capital to the labour market and mass consumption" (7–15).

Clandfield's public advocacy of community hub schools carries considerable weight in Canadian progressive education reform circles. Although little known in Nova Scotia, he is an influential Ontario progressive reformer, who served as Ontario NDP Education Minister Tony Silipo's chief policy advisor from 1991 to 1993. His proposal for transforming schools into community hubs is grounded in the British settlement house movement and focuses on closing the socio-economic gap in urban inner city communities. It starts, not surprisingly, with a commitment to building-in daycare services and "best start" early learning programs like that recommended by Charles Pascal in 2009, now one of the foundational components of the Ontario school system (14, 29–33).

Clandfield also strongly favours utilizing hub schools to break down the educational silos and advance "intergenerational learning." In recasting children's education with adult education providers and seniors groups as key partners, alongside public health and family services, the new model offers fresh opportunities to systematically alleviate poverty as well as a wider span of learning activities, ranging from financial literacy to arts appreciation. Such full service schools also provide a place for immigrant and newcomer services and even community gardens, once the cornerstone of outdoor activities for rural schoolchildren in both Ontario and Nova Scotia (33–58).

The "community hub school" has the look of what Clandfield aptly describes as "a politician's dream," but it is also an elusive concept of schooling, subject to ambiguity and fuzziness. He is helpful in situating true community hubs on a five-point continuum from the traditional community use of schools to a fully integrated school-community relationship, considered a true hub. Transforming schools into community hubs means moving away from strict "community use of schools" practices to "co-location" of services and finally to the ideal of a "two-way" community hub school. In his formulation, granting access to schools after hours is a manifestation of market-driven priorities rather than evidence of cultural transformation in the school community. That transformation is "local" in an intentional way and builds upon the sense of community found in a city neighbourhood, village, or small town (19–21).

Clandfield is a social democratic visionary and an idealist who sees the community hub as a prime vehicle for reconstructing the social order. His ideal full community hub would harness "the interactive neighbourhood school with the multi-use hub to

Dr. David Clandfield put "community hub schools" on the public policy agenda with the publication in 2010 of "The School as a Community Hub," in Our Schools Our Selves. A former French professor at the University of Toronto, he is a committed education reformer long associated with the Canadian Centre for Policy Alternatives.

produce a kind of New Commons where education for all, health, recreation, poverty reduction, cultural expression and celebration, and environmental responsibility can all come together" (21). It is here, he believes, where a sense of community flourishes, forged on "principles of citizenship, co-operation and social justice." He is dead set against private or alternative schools in Canada's urban communities and sees the community hub school as a way of countering their increasing popularity and stopping the creep of "neoliberal globalization" forces in the public education sphere. It is not as clear how he would view the rural Nova Scotian situation, where children and parents confront an essentially unitary school system, with few if any choices, narrowly circumscribed by "hard, uncrossable boundaries" that limit the range of educational provision. Here urban boutique schools are virtually unknown and the only real item on the standard school menu is what he would term "fast food for the many" (21–23).

Nova Scotia's Education Minister Ramona Jennex is fond of describing the Nova Scotia SchoolsPlus model as a provincial community school initiative. This model, in theory and in practice, is actually designed to serve a specific student population and falls far short of Clandfield's definition of a true community hub school concept. On his five-point continuum, it falls into the second category, representing a modest variation on traditional community use of school practices. An independent research report on the working of Nova Scotia's SchoolsPlus from 2008 to 2013 demonstrates that it has become essentially a means of bringing centralized, regional services into the schools, at limited times under controlled conditions (Bennett 2013b). Integrating centralized child, youth, and family services into the schools (as is the case with the Nova Scotia SchoolsPlus model) is only a small part of the equation. A true community hub is a genuine partnership; it is built around the schools and draws far more upon local, volunteer, and community enterprise.

What Schools Mean to Small Rural Communities

Schools research is beginning to address the fundamental challenges posed by rural school closures and the enormous potential of transforming schools into community hubs. A team of Australian researchers, sponsored by Rural Industries Research and Development Corporation (RIRDC 2002) and based at the University of Tasmania, laid the groundwork with a report focusing on the development of social capital in Australia's declining rural areas. Based upon case studies of five rural communities, the researchers discovered the critical importance of effective leadership, particularly in cementing the school-community partnerships so instrumental in building community social capital. Faced with an external threat, marked by the closure of rural banks and other services, community leaders surfaced both in the school and outside to forge new partnerships across traditional functional lines and then develop hard visions that met their collective needs and goals.

School and community leadership make the difference and, in its absence, schools and villages perish in rural areas. Driven by self-preservation but committed to changing the trend lines, community leaders in Australia transformed a dire threat into a fleeting opportunity. The RIRDC study identified five stages of initiation: trigger, initiation, development, maintenance, and sustainability. The schools studied survived because they successfully generated school-community partnerships and came to offer "more than an education." A different kind of school leadership was required, one that went well beyond the traditional role of "maintaining boundaries" around the school. Joint leadership and power-sharing proved crucial for the "development, maintenance, and sustainability stages of the partnership" as the initiative gradually came to be "owned by the community" (ix–xii, 122–30).

Failure to intervene in defence of threatened rural schools can have devastating consequences for their communities. Closer to home, Dr. Thomas A. Lyson, a Cornell University sociologist, provides disturbing evidence of that impact, based upon his studies in upstate New York of rural communities with populations of 500 or less and towns with between 501 and 2,500 inhabitants.

As a leading expert on American school consolidation, he is clearly aware of the larger trends and profoundly influenced by the work of Alan Peshkin in the late 1970s and early 1980s. "Viable villages generally contain schools; dying and dead ones either lack them or do not have them for long.… The capacity to maintain a school is a continuing indicator of a community's well-being" Peshkin observed over twenty-five years ago. That finding is what prompted Lyson to dig a little deeper and to determine what having a school actually means to a rural village and small town (Lyson 2002: 131).

Lyson's research makes a convincing case that school consolidation has been, and continues to be, a detriment to the viability and quality of rural education. The reputed advantages of consolidation on student academic performance, he insisted, are "greatly outweighed by the disadvantages," including the "deleterious effects" on educational quality, student performance, and the economic viability of small rural communities. Schools prove to be absolutely essential social anchors in the rural New York villages and any reported savings through consolidation were "forfeited in lost taxes, declining property values, and lost businesses." Villages retaining schools also show higher rates of civic engagement, less income inequality, and fewer cases of welfare dependence. Such findings even prompted the New York State government, following a State Environmental Quality Review, to financially

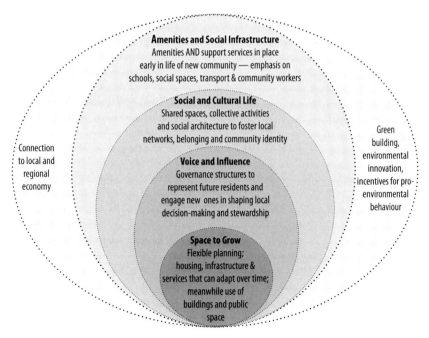

The Young Foundation, based in the U.K., produced this illustration of the concept of a social sustainability framework for local and regional planning.

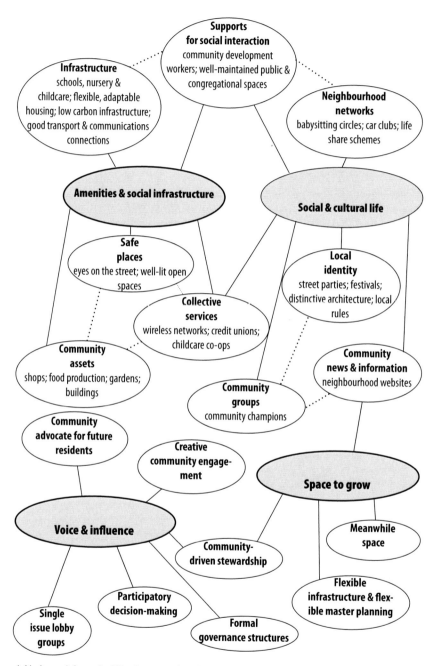

Achieving social sustainability in community planning and development requires a focus on four inter-related aspects: amenities and social infrastructure, social and cultural life, space to grow, and voice and influence. When all are present communities grow and thrive. (Young Foundation)

compensate villages for suffering the loss of their school. Rural communities that are thriving are the ones with schools, and they are also places where "the citizenry is civically engaged, local businesses prosper, and those factors anchor populations in place." In the case of New York's smallest rural villages, Lyson found that "schools serve as important markers of social and economic viability and vitality" (135–36).

Community sustainability is no longer considered simply a matter of geographic location, demographic trends, and the dictates of the market. City and town planners in Britain, the United States and Western Canada are actually beginning to design communities with a consistent, coherent approach rooted in a philosophy of social sustainability and a set of design principles at odds with the "bigger is better" mindset of private developers and school facilities planners. Learning from their past mistakes, British town planners are gradually adopting a new framework and "designing in" the latest ideas aimed at enabling dormitory suburbs and townscapes to become more socially sustainable as well as economically viable.

While designing in social sustainability is gaining acceptance among city and town planners, it remains, for the most part, unknown among provincial school planners and school board facilities managers. Designing smaller schools better suited to smaller communities makes perfect sense, and so does adopting the approach and practices of leading building design and home building firms now far more sensitive to what it takes to sustain healthy, socially responsible, economically thriving communities. The Social Sustainability Framework, espoused by the Young Foundation, could well be applied in looking more broadly at situating schools within communities instead of as outward extensions of a centrally managed school system. Taking schools off the endangered buildings list and allowing them to run-down further is no longer defensible when new and more creative options are available and right around the corner.

The Rise of the Community Hub Movement

New and exciting ideas are surfacing as a result of inspiring community enterprise and local community-led initiatives. The recent round of Nova Scotia school reviews, conducted in three school boards during 2012–13, produced some of those pleasant surprises. Once popular myths about "bigger is better" consolidation ventures were exploded by a steady procession of speakers at every public hearing in almost every one of the fourteen schools under review for closure. Over and over again, school board members were harangued and schooled on the finer points of small school research, best educational practice, and plain common sense. The common public refrain, repeated over two dozen times: Small schools are living examples of "personalized learning," which is not just the theme for a cutting edge professional development program. Renovating small schools is far more cost effective than building new oversized facilities with the overblown capital, infrastructure, and transportation costs factored in. Local taxpayers do not ultimately win when the costs of maintaining or disposing of abandoned schools are downloaded onto rural municipalities. Putting children aged four to ten on buses for two to three hours a day is not only unhealthy but puts them at higher risk of bullying and is nonsensical in the digital age.

Public hearings in the small rural villages of Petite Riviere, Maitland, and River John turned out virtually the entire community. Speaker after speaker asked: who here is actually in favour of "big box" elementary proposals and busing elementary kids to these distant schools? The answer: no one, except perhaps for battle-worn board staff suffering in silence. The Petite Plus vision, created by Leif Helmer and Dee Conrad, at Petite Riviere Elementary School on the South Shore, became something of a catalyst. The Study Committee's February 1, 2013, report set a new standard by going well beyond simply rejecting the school closure agenda promulgated in the SSRSB's impact assessment reports, produced by Dr. Jim Gunn, now freshly minted as a Halifax-based Deloitte management consultant. It not only offered a constructive solution to the Petite Riviere problem but ventured into new territory, suggesting a completely different strategy to address declining enrolments across the entire school district.

The Maitland Plan, developed by Cathrine Yuill and her School Study Committee, gained critical support from Kevin Quinlan, Principal of NSCC Truro and chair of the Coastal Communities Network. With the quiet sup-

A watercolour by Christopher Gill captures the Petite Rivière Community Hub vision, February 2013.

port of the local principal, Yuill and her committee proposed to open the school to community partnerships and lease excess space to NSCC Truro for continuing education programs, expand Boy Scout activities, and serve as a base for CHARTS, the East Hants arts festival group. Local parents besieged CCRSB Chair Trudy Thompson, a Maitland resident, turning thumbs down on a proposal to buy the parents off with the promise of a "big box" school an hour away on country back roads. Most significant of all, the Maitland group acknowledged that their school, with only twenty-five students, must be transformed into a community hub school to have any chance of surviving and to secure its future sustainability.

The River John Study Committee, led by the feisty Abby Taylor, was initially caught off-guard by the determination of the CCRSB to move ahead with school closure. Outraged by the impact assessment report plan to close the school and bus seventy-six students in different directions, Taylor rallied her entire besieged community for what looked much like a "last stand" against the central administration down in Truro. After developing a local community hub model, the School Study Committee secured the return of the RCMP office, local film-maker FLAWed Productions, and the SCORE Pre-School program. A month later, on February 28, 2013, a crowd numbering over 287 residents packed the River John School Gym and unified behind the community hub plan. Maritime children's author Sheree Fitch, a River John resident, joined the long speakers' lineup and spoke with characteristic passion about her commitment to keeping the school open. The community spirit generated by the River John project was hailed in March 2013 as a visible sign of rural regeneration on the Northumberland Shore (Mackenzie 2013).

If the community hub movement continues to spread, it will be because of the public advocacy of committed and determined small schoolers like Leif Helmer, Catherine Yuill, and Abby Taylor during 2012–13. That movement can be traced back to its origins in a brainstorming session held December 12, 2012, in a Tim Horton's coffee shop in Bridgewater on a cold winter's night. The Petite Plus vision, hatched that night, became the most adventuresome and exciting plan, embracing innovation, local artists, and videoconferencing. With a $2 million renovation, the Petite Plus plan was designed to save local taxpayers between $6 million and $8 million of the cost of a new large elementary school. It offered a viable third option, broke new ground in Nova Scotia public education, and showed great promise. Helmer's public advocacy efforts aroused hope for those resisting the relentless tide of centralization, consolidation, and rural school abandonment in Nova Scotia.

School closure battles in 2012–13 came to a head in March of 2013 as three boards, CCRSB, SSRSB, and TCRSB, were required, under the school review process, to make decisions on the future of fourteen schools. The Chignecto-Central Regional School Board was first out of the gate on March

20, 2013. Two schools proposing the option of becoming a community hub school, Maitland District School and River John Consolidated School, were each given two years (until 2015) to produce a viable business plan or face closure. The Wentworth Study Committee was challenged to come up with a community hub proposal and given a one-year stay of execution, or it would be closed in 2014. Historic Bass River Elementary School, spared in 2010 and in the midst of its hundredth anniversary year, was voted to be closed in June 2013. Thirteen of seventeen CCRSB board members voted to support the Maitland community hub plan but gave Cathrine Yuill a firm deadline of June 1015 to put the plan in place. A shift in attitudes was detected, and the school board members appeared more inclined to put their trust in communities to come up with their own plans for school sustainability. New Glasgow member Jamie Stevens president of the Nova Scotia School Boards Association, argued that closing schools did not make good sense, while Ray Ivany and his Economic Commission were touring the province looking for ways to rejuvenate rural Nova Scotia. "I think it would be short-sighted of us," Stevens stated, "to close small schools to meet our budget deadlines" (Gorman 2013).

Hopes soared early the next week when the *Chronicle Herald* published a three-part series of feature articles entitled "Schools Under Siege" in rural Nova Scotia. The in-depth reports, researched and written by education reporter Frances Willick, seemed to represent a breakthrough, raising the profile of the school closure issue throughout HRM and all over the province. The first report featured the Maitland School, southwest of Truro, in the Chignecto-Regional Board, which demonstrates the true value of "personalized learning" in a school with twenty-six Primary to Grade 5 students occupying a well-maintained eight-room school, located one to one and a half hours each way by bus from its nearest school. Teacher Nicole Graham made a persuasive case for keeping the school open. "I love this school," she told Willick, "I love the children. You get to know them so well.... Everyone who needs to be challenged is challenged, and everyone who needs that little extra is getting it."

The Nova Scotia school review process came under the microscope in the second installment. Small school advocate Jens Laursen, a veteran of the bitter 2011 Riverport School closure battle, provided personal testimony on the energy sapping review process and the futile attempt of the Parent Focus Group to secure improvements during a 2008–09 provincial moratorium. Bitterness and frustration were expressed by Wentworth School Study Committee Chair Cecil McLeod, a professional roofer stonewalled in his attempt to remedy, at no cost, the deferred maintenance in his son's school. The closure of Rev. J.H. MacDonald School in Heatherton, for a reported saving of $160,000, Willick reported, sparked Denise Delorey and a parent group to launch an unsuccessful $10,000 law suit, only to discover, six months later, that $3.5 million was being spent to upgrade the receiving school in the Town of Antigonish. Education consultant Paul Bennett insisted that, travelling the backroads while researching this book, he had witnessed, first hand, "a School Review Process that was, at root, divisive" and one leaving a legacy, over and over again, of "lasting scars." The piece closed with this succinct assessment: "They're not closing schools; they're shutting down communities."

Community hub schools were presented, in Willick's last feature story, as an innovative idea which may give small schools "a new lease on life." South Shore United Church minister Vivian Moores drew a stark and powerfully moving distinction between Petite Riviere, with its own school, and Riverport, a sadly beaten community that lost its school in June 2011. Leif Helmer, father of two young kids at Petite Riviere Elementary School, made a compelling case for the Petite Plus plan, which embraces the community hub school philosophy. He outlined the school renewal and expansion plan, incorporating the South Shore public libraries, the Lunenburg County YMCA, South Shore Health, and the Municipality of Lunenburg. Spending $1.5 million to $2 million on renovating the school, he pointed out, was far more reasonable than sinking millions more into a new school down the road. Interviewed for the story, Education Minister Ramona Jennex disclosed, for the first time, that she was warming to "the idea of community hubs."

That high-profile *Chronicle Herald* series raised high hopes that were soon dashed. Traditional school board ways and thinking die hard. On the same day the series ended, March 27, 2013, the South Shore Regional School Board rendered its decisions on the fate of six more schools. At that critical meeting, the eight-person elected board claimed that balancing the SSRSB budget could only be achieved by closing schools, thus covering a $1.8 million shortfall in the coming year (Ware 2013a). After an intense, on and off again, internal debate stretching over an entire weekend, they rejected the Petite Plus plan and decided to merge Petite Riviere Elementary School with Pentz Elementary School, fifteen kilometres away, in a proposed future school located between the two villages. Two other small rural schools were also slated for closure, Gold River-Western Shore Elementary School, in June 2013, and Mill Village Consolidated School, a year later, in June 2014. In line with the Gunn grade reconfiguration plan, the board also moved Grade 9s from New Ross Consolidated to Forest Heights Community School, housing Grades 9 to 12. While Mill Village was given a year-long reprieve, the tiny school lost its Grade 6 students, further weakening its student enrolment (Ware 2013a).

Following the tense March 27, 2013, meeting there was no joy in Hebbville. The hopes generated by the Willick series and Petite Plus suffered a significant setback. The South Shore Board, following a familiar routine, had simply moved a series of standard closure motions, making only passing reference to the community hub plan and suggesting it for the future new school. Helmer was visibly shaken by the rebuff, especially when his School Study Committee co-chair Dee Conrad essentially gave up the fight and quickly jumped into line on the appeal of a new school sometime in the future. The morning after, Helmer was disconsolate, predicting "years more of uncertainty" because a promised "new build" twelve kilometres away for 160 to 170 students was not likely to even happen. His biggest fear was that the province would deny funding, leaving Petite and Pentz elementary kids on those long bus rides to Hebbville Academy, the scene of that painful night of reckoning (Leif Helmer email, March 28, 2013). Time would tell whether it would be another missed opportunity for rural and small town Nova Scotia.

Just when the clouds appeared to be gathering, Nova Scotia's widely read newspaper came to the rescue. On Good Friday, March 29, 2013, the *Chronicle Herald* published an editorial endorsing the Schools at the Centre vision and proposing community hubs as the preferred approach to revitalizing rural schools and communities. A trenchant political cartoon, produced by Bruce Mackinnon, showed a gloomy Premier Darrell Dexter gathered around the Cabinet table beside a blackboard showing a Big X through the posted topic, "School Closure & Review Process." The editorial, entitled "Small School Closures: Think Bigger," provided a succinct and persuasive case, aimed at the premier and his cabinet:

Gut-Wrenching and Mind-Boggling

That's how the school-closure process feels to those parents, children, small communities — and even board officials — on the receiving end. That's what our news coverage has so vividly captured from anger-filled public meetings across Nova Scotia this week as the fate of those beloved buildings that find themselves in the precarious zone hangs in the balance. That's also what stands out in Education Reporter Frances Willick's outstanding three-part series on the small-school conundrum, which concluded on Wednesday.

Whether or not a school is saved, the universal feeling about the process is that the government is working against regular folks.

But the underlying reality is that the government is often working at cross-purposes with itself when it comes to small rural schools.

On the one hand, we have the Department of Education man-dating cuts that are driven by declining enrolment and the need to balance the provincial budget. School boards, in turn, must figure out where to allocate and reallocate resources, from teachers to buildings.

On the other hand, we have the Department of Economic and

Rural Development trying to figure out, among other things, how to sustain rural communities. Often, the pillar of those communities is the small, local school. After it's gone and the kids are bused out, parents may be tempted to move to the larger centre too, to spare the kids the drudgery of the daily commute. Meanwhile, the absence of a school within walking distance in the community they left behind hampers efforts to attract newcomers and their families. Professionals with young children are prized economic assets that should be nurtured, not neutered.

Rural residents understand this well, which is why the "community hub" concept is being touted as a natural survival strategy. "Under this model," Ms. Willick writes, "schools throw open their doors to non-profits, community organizations, businesses, municipal offices and government services, which lease the space.... Rental agreements generate revenue that's needed by cash-strapped school boards. The new tenants help fill the space that's deemed 'excess' by school boards."

Not every small school can be saved through this kind of ingenuity. Some, it is sad to say, should be closed because their existence and expense can no longer be justified. But potential hub schools that can cobble together a sound business plan should get a reprieve from their respective school boards and perhaps even assistance in various forms, where necessary, from the province. The latter could pay for repairs or lease space. No one cares whether the dollars are extracted from the silo of Economic Development rather than Education if the long-term viability of the community is at stake.

That editorial provided all the incentive Nova Scotia small schoolers needed to not only keep up the good fight but to exert even more public pressure on the premier to act by suspending the school review process and embrace the community hub model as a viable option for rural revitalization.

Putting facilities first was losing its appeal and the Small Schools Initiative seemed to be winning the war of public opinion. Closing the small schools was creating a harvest of bitterness in school after school and was making school boards' claims that they were really interested in building "learning communities" increasingly less credible. A third option was slowly emerging as the best way forward because it challenged school communities themselves to come together, to develop their own community hub plan, and to breathe new life into public education. Thinking small, dreaming bigger, opening the doors, and turning small schools into community hubs was now surfacing, from the ground up, as the wave of the near future.

Signs of Hope, Solidarity and Resilience

"Small schools produce great citizens." — Slogan on "KIDS, not Cut$" Protest Flag, Weymouth, NS, March 8, 2012

"Gut Wrenching and mind-boggling. That's how the school closure process feels to those parents, children, small communities — and even board officials — on the receiving end.… Rural residents understand … [the problem of the population drain] well, which is why the 'community hub' concept is being touted as a natural survival strategy." — "Small School Closures: Think Bigger," editorial, *Chronicle Herald,* March 27, 2013

Fighting to save small rural schools is a rollercoaster ride for small school advocates, for whom small victories loom large and help to stiffen the backbone. One of those David and Goliath struggles that inspires rural education reformers was the local battle from October 2011 until March 2012 to save Weymouth Consolidated School on the outer reaches of Digby County on Nova Scotia's Southwest shore. It was a classic struggle to save Weymouth's prized community asset and centre of rural community life (Medel 2011). The closer you look at the community, the more clear it becomes how important their public school is to the village's very survival.

Flashback: The 2011 Weymouth School Uprising

For a small village on the Sissiboo River, officially founded by Loyalists in 1783, Weymouth Consolidated School, with 242 students from Primary to Grade 6 in 2011–12, is the social anchor for the whole community. The village, inhabited by 1,173 people (2011), straddles the Sissiboo River near St. Mary's Bay. It is a border village, near the boundary between Digby County and neighbouring Clare, a predominantly Acadian French county. Situated where it is, the village might be considered relatively isolated, even though it is only 33 kilometres from the Town of Digby and some 72 kilometres from Yarmouth. It is surrounded by even smaller villages, such as Weymouth Falls, Weaver Settlement, Ohio, Southville, Riverdale, Danvers, Hassett, Saint

Bernard, and New Edinburgh. It is accessible by two exits on Nova Scotia Highway 101 and sits on the old highway now described as Main Street, Weymouth.

Typical of most Nova Scotia villages, Weymouth is suffering a slow demographic decline. Based on the 2011 Census, Weymouth had a population of 1,773, which was 8.0 percent lower than in 2001. In 2011, 22.0 percent of the population was under the age of twenty and 20.9 percent was sixty-five years or older. The total number of families had decreased by 8.0 percent, to 545, between 2006 and 2011. Married families decreased by 3.5 percent while common law families decreased by 31.0 percent and lone-parent families by 31.0 percent. Lone female parent families were 12.7 percent of all families while lone male parents were only 3.3 percent of all families. Some 90.5 percent of Weymouth residents speak English in the home, while 13.5 percent claim French as their mother tongue. While 22 percent of the population is under twenty years of age, the figure drops to 12.2 percent for ages twenty to thirty-four, indicating that large numbers of Weymouth's born and bred leave in their twenties, perhaps never to return (Nova Scotia Government 2013).

When the school was identified for possible closure, Weymouth was struggling economically, and so were most of its residents. In 2006, the most recent data available, the median income for individuals in Weymouth was $18,923 a year, compared with the median of $24,030 for Nova Scotia. Families in Weymouth had a median income of $39,240, compared with the median of $55,412 for Nova Scotia. Median household income, according to Community Counts, was only $31,328, or 76 percent of the provincial average, second lowest in Digby County. A total of 13.6 percent of families in Weymouth were classified as low income status in 2006, compared with 10.3 percent of families across the whole province (Nova Scotia Government 2013).

For a relatively poor little community, Weymouth demonstrated plenty of spunk in resisting the threatened school closure. Shortly after the school was identified by the Tri-County Regional School Board, based in Yarmouth, parent Jamie Lewis formed the Coalition to Save Weymouth Consolidated School. "There's a lot of people who don't want to see us lose that school," Lewis told the *Chronicle Herald's* Southwest Bureau reporter Brian Medel. He was not exaggerating. Within several weeks of its launch, in late October 2011, the Save Weymouth Facebook site had 850 followers and some 2,500 flyers had been sent out around the area seeking support. The TCRSB plan to close Weymouth School and bus all 242 kids to an expanded St. Mary's Bay Academy went over like a lead balloon. A school board report claiming that closing the school, a 45,000 square foot facility, and building a six room, 10,000 sq. ft. addition to St. Mary's Bay Academy would save $120,000 a year was disputed by the parents. Local MLA Harold (Junior) Theriault was in their corner and so was the Nova Scotia Association of Mink Breeders, who leased a portion of the Weymouth School for their operations (Medel 2011; Comeau 2011; Riley 2012).

The Weymouth March and Rally

Frustration and anger grew as the Save Weymouth Consolidated School campaign wore on and the TCRSB prepared for the public hearing, scheduled for March 8, 2012. Local businessman Larry Donald Haight, president of the Weymouth Board of Trade, spearheaded the community protest, turning his tiny office into the headquarters, complete with flyers and stacks of homemade signs and little flags. An hour before the hearing, a sizeable crowd of marchers gathered in the village square and marched over a kilometre against a stiff, bone chilling wind, and uphill to the public hearing at the school. When the meeting started, Board Chair Donna Tidd and the assembled elected board gazed out at gymnasium packed with Save Weymouth supporters of all ages, from infants to grandparents. Community leaders, business owners, ministers, and a whole row of mink farmers occupied the seats, bearing bristol board signs and tiny flags saying "KIDS, not cut$." The elected board members hid behind the school review process, offering no comments, and sat stone-faced as they listened for over two hours to eighteen or more people, including a couple of children, make passionate appeals to save their school (Medel 2012).

Larry Haight delivered the critical blow to the TCRSB's business case for closing the school. Since December of 2012, he had been picking apart the impact assessment report, taking direct aim at the rationale and the lack of supporting financial data. The TCRSB, he found, had not done its homework. He discovered that, over the previous eight years, WCS was the only school

The marchers congregate in Weymouth village square preparing for the protest parade to Weymouth Consolidated School for the packed Public Hearing in March 2012. (Photo: Karla Kelly)

in the entire board region that had increased its enrolment. He also claimed that no "pedagogically sound" reason had been given for sending students to a Primary to Grade 12 school and that property service costs were going to be 15.27 percent higher per square foot in the receiving school. The road blocks set up to try to deny his access to the relevant data only added to his fierce determination to derail the board's real game plan.

All eyes were on Haight at the public hearing when he finally took the microphone. Calmly and rationally, he addressed the underlying issue of school board secrecy and fear of accountability. At a time when Tri-County school board administration were on the lookout for student bullies, he charged that senior staff were stonewalling and using bully-boy tactics to fend off inquiring parents. "The review of our school has been a bullying process from the beginning," he stated bluntly. "There is no justifiable reason to consider our school for review or to put this community through this trauma.… The total lack of response from board members to the hundreds of emails and letters from community members is appalling." When the thunderous applause died down after his presentation, Study Committee Chair Jamie Lewis put it all in perspective. Too many questions had been raised without receiving any sound or plausible answers from the Yarmouth Board Office. "There's so much evidence … to support not closing the school that everybody is just sort of saying: 'How can they think they should close it?'" (Medel 2012).

Save our School kids were the first to arrive at the public hearing to decide the fate of Weymouth Consolidated School in March 2012. (Private collection)

The elected Tri-County Regional School Board absorbed all of the public flack and voted on March 27, 2012, to abandon the field. The very next day, a post popped up on the Save Weymouth Consolidated Facebook page: "Weymouth School Saved — Community Lives." It was a very sweet little victory for local citizen democracy, but Lewis and Haight were under no illusions. It was likely merely a reprieve and the true lesson learned was never to take your eye off that regional school board making decisions affecting your children 72 kilometres distant and a world away in Yarmouth. Endurance tests like the Weymouth school closure battle leave a few bruises and tend to teach real life lessons in community resilience.

Save Small Schools, Revitalize Small Communities

Closing small schools administers a terrible blow to rural communities because local schools are an important part of the glue that holds communities together. They are the new social anchor — whether it be for parents coming together at fall rituals like the ice cream socials, Brownies meeting in the gym after school hours, or Elections Nova Scotia using schools as polling booths. The closure of a school is devastating to small towns, remote communities, and villages alike. It often leads to the whole district's slow decline, as families and teachers move away and marginal businesses close (Dare and Bennett 2011; Gill 2012a; Willick 2013).

The macabre school closure scorecard is indicative of the downward spiral. From 2007 until 2012, a five-year period, some forty-three public schools were identified for possible closure, twenty-one of which were in the sprawling Chignecto-Central School Board district (Willick 2013). The most recent wave of closures presented the latest crisis for many smaller communities. But the written word for "crisis" in Chinese consists of two characters — one representing danger and the other representing opportunity. Looking on the brighter side, the school closure crisis in fact offered the premier, the Department of Education and school boards an opportunity; it also sparked the formation of the Nova Scotia Small Schools Initiative and led to the publication of this book.

What's the best way forward for Nova Scotia? It begins by adopting a wider community development lens –and re-thinking the central administrator's view of schools as big boxes dedicated solely to the education of children. Viewed within the narrow lens, schools with declining enrolments are seen as liabilities instead of community assets. If the Education Department clings to this view, then there is no possible path other than closing dozens of schools. But if we are prepared to think flexibly about schools, we can solve their excess capacity problems and in the process achieve better schools.

We need to look at the unused space in schools in a different way. Nova Scotia's Schools Plus initiative is only one possible approach and it will be

The 2013 moratorium simply asked school boards to suspend the closure process. When the Tri-County Regional School Board rebuffed that request, Save Rural Schools Yarmouth, led by Janessa Blauvelt and John Levac, picketed the Board Office under the sign reading "Students First," the TCRSB's official motto. (Tina Comeau, The Vanguard)

found unequal to the challenge. It is far too narrowly circumscribed and does not even address the central question — re-engineering day schools and converting the surviving schools into community development centres. The mandate of this provincial initiative is also limited to serving the 5 to 10 percent of students at highest risk of dropping-out of school and either falling by the wayside or drifting into a life of criminal activities (NSSBA 2010; Bennett 2013b).

The Schools Plus initiative looks like another "add-on" program that does not really address the fundamental challenges facing rural education. Properly implemented, it might make money by renting or selling the unused space to family service agencies offering complementary services. It falls short in every other aspect because it does not embrace the fundamental principle of rural community development — the Schools at the Centre model of rural revitalization and development.

Embracing a public engagement model will open the door to new and innovative ideas. Why not consider more creative solutions, such as renting the unused school space to generate extra income? What about selling off some of the "white elephant" big boxes and moving the remaining students to a non-traditional space in the same neighbourhood? An independent school partnership is another obvious choice, and the two schools could co-operate in various ways — for example, sharing buses or maintaining an outdoor skating rink in winter.

Selling off some of the big box schools is not as outlandish as it sounds. Most Nova Scotians clearly favour small schools, so why not provide schooling in smaller, less expensive venues like church basements, community centres, or unused commercial space? If schools were relocated to a local church, or the wing of a community college, just think of the possibilities for enriched athletics, providing extra music lessons, or adult evening programs. Do all schools really need principals, when the Swiss education system functions without them? And even Tim Horton's has accepted the need for alternative supervisory models in small villages, with part-time managers responsible for two or three outlets (Dare and Bennett 2011).

For many rural schools with shrinking enrolments, the community hub model should have considerable appeal. It starts by accepting that the regular day school will have to occupy a smaller footprint inside the existing building, in keeping with student numbers. Once the actual required space is determined, then community groups with compatible social functions, serving inter-generational groups, can and should be invited to share in occupying the space and in contributing to the development of more diverse, community-based offering of programs for kids and adults alike. Forming a cooperative among the community groups and developing a business plan are the next logical steps in transforming the school facility into a genuine Community Hub school (Elliott 2011; Helmer 2013).

The current Nova Scotia public school system represents, in its many guises, the highest stage of the bureaucratic education state. School consolidation is ingrained in the thinking of education authorities and reflects the continuing domination of facilities planning principles in the provision of state schooling. Centralized administration, the regionalization of high schools, and the spread of "big box" elementary schools are but the outward expressions of a command and control system that continues to threaten small schools and struggling rural communities. Suspending the school review process and halting the closure of small schools in April 2013 was a positive sign that the voices of rural Nova Scotia are, for once, being heard in the inner sanctum of Nova Scotia government. The idea of transforming small schools into community hub schools has gained currency with the minister of education and all three of Nova Scotia's political parties. To make it work will require a significant shift in the direction of community-building and the embracing of a more grounded, rurally attuned curriculum reflecting a fuller commitment to rural regeneration and sustainability.

Nova Scotia's daily newspaper, the *Chronicle Herald*, has urged the provincial government, Education Department and school boards to embrace "new model schools," which will deliver public education on a smaller, more efficient, and networked fashion befitting the twenty-first-century world. School consolidation and centralized administration are being challenged by

Nova Scotians, urban and rural, seeking a more responsive public education system delivered on what Michael Corbett and Dennis Mulcahy have aptly termed "a more human scale." Declaring a provincial moratorium on the school review process was hailed by the paper on April 4, 2013, as the right move, ending the divisive exercise that had degenerated into "a dysfunctional trial" and opening the door to "a fairer more collaborative process." If it amounted only to a temporary cessation for electoral advantage, then the *Herald* editorial board sees it as a missed opportunity. "What is a step forward," they emphasize, "is a commitment to come up with some models and criteria for the hub concept, or for other collaborative approaches to delivering education in small settings, that communities are genuinely eager to adopt."

The Nova Scotia school review process is now on "pause," but *The Last Stand* issues a clarion call for a complete change in direction. Out of the divisive and punishing school closure crisis, an opportunity may materialize to create new and better schools for rural and small town Nova Scotians. Public hearings over school closures are adversarial and divisive endurance tests when they could be reinvented as community engagement exercises rebuilding relations and blazing the trail for rural development and more sustainable communities. Simply closing small rural schools when enrolment shrinks and moving children to distant regional education centres will consign far too many rural communities to a bleak future.

Suspending the school review process for 2013–14 should buy some re-thinking time, allow Nova Scotians to confront this silent, unrelenting process, and encourage the province to take the lead in a project aimed at re-inventing our current model of schooling for the twenty-first century. Building rejuvenated rural communities should start in the schools, tapping into the communitarian spirit, local initiative, and social enterprise resident in our too often forgotten rural spaces. Transforming threatened small schools into community hubs could well be the start of rural regeneration and open the door to a much brighter future.

Appendix A

Schools at the Centre Vision and Recommendations (May 15, 2012)

Closing small schools is not a winning formula for rural and small town Nova Scotia. It's a terrible blow to rural communities when they lose their school, because local schools are an important part of the glue that holds communities together. The closure of a school is devastating to small towns, remote communities and villages alike. It often leads to the whole district's slow decline, as families and teachers move away and marginal businesses close as a result.

Hidden deep inside the school closure crisis is the opportunity to create new and better schools. Simply closing community schools when enrolment shrinks and moving children to distant regional education centres will consign rural communities to a bleak future. Suspending the school review process would allow Nova Scotians to confront this silent, unrelenting process and to take the lead in a project aimed at re-inventing our current model of schooling for the 21st century. A new model of schooling is emerging — the Community Hub School — and it's a project with the promise of hope and revitalization.

Key Recommendations

We call upon the Minister of Education to take the lead in addressing the looming crisis affecting rural and small town Nova Scotia, signalled by the latest round of small school closures and their potentially devastating consequences for what remains of rural life.

The Small School Delegation, composed of activists for all parts of Nova Scotia, recommends a province-wide strategy seeking to arrest the disturbing trend and to provide rural communities with a reason for hope in the 21st century.

It is recommended that:

1. The Minister of Education take the lead in advancing the *Kids & Learning First* plan by embracing a *Community School at the Centre* philosophy aimed at revitalizing rural education through a province-wide, community-building and development strategy. Instead of abandoning small schools

to a School Review for closure process, move schools to the centre of planning for the future.

2. The Minister announce a Moratorium on the School Review process, covering all schools identified in the current provincial cycle of school accommodation reviews. Such a move would send a powerful signal that the current School Review process is broken, acknowledging that it's adversarial, divisive, destroys confidence in the public system — and needs to be re-examined as a go-forward strategy.

3. The Minister and Department take the lead in developing a Rural Revitalization Strategy, working with Economic and Rural Development, and generated though a public engagement process involving all interested groups, including school boards, regional development agencies, school councils, teachers, local boards of trade, local government and citizens.

4. A Rural Education and Development Strategy take precedence over a School Review process in charting the future of rural and small town Nova Scotia. A one-year moratorium on school closures would provide a "time-out" and focus our energies on exploring and developing community-based alternative approaches.

5. The Minister and the Department consider the advantages of adopting a Public Engagement Model in place of the current quasi-judicial School Review process seeking to find community-based solutions and rendering most, if not all, School Reviews unnecessary exercises. Such a Model could actually run in tandem with, and be fully integrated with, Community Development Plans.

6. A Ministerial Review be initiated fully examining the Education Act and Regulations as they relate to school reviews, with a view to levelling the playing field by shifting the *burden of proof* to those seeking school shutdowns. Instead of simply bolstering School Review Committees, raise the bar for school boards so that the process is reserved as a strategy of last resort.

7. Build on the *Nova Scotia Virtual School* project by initiating a Rural Schools Online Education Network, based upon the Newfoundland model, creating digitally-networked schools and taking fuller advantage of distance education in the 21st century guise of virtual schooling. Seek amendments to the Education Act and the collective agreements to remove obstacles to providing blended online and regular learning programs in rural and remote parts of the province.

8. The Minister and Department act on the *Kids & Learning First* commitment to safeguard small schools in rural and remote parts of the province Instead of closing small schools and plowing rural communities under, provide the longer-term strategy critical for rural community survival

and sustainability. Generate a Rural Strategy, modelled after that of Manitoba and Ontario, resting on the fundamental pillars of Schools at the Centre, Community Partnerships, ICT Innovation, and Sustainable Economic and Social Development.

9. The Minister take a role in facilitating the partnerships necessary to help small rural communities turn their schools into multi-use buildings. (Or something of this nature... I have been told by different gov. people that this is the way of the future, but as a citizen, I have no idea where to start, this seems to be something that requires local input, but has to be done at the provincial/municipal level.)

Small Schools Delegation

List of Members, May 2012

Annapolis Valley Region

    Michael Corbett, School of Education, Acadian University

    Steven Rhude, Wolfville Elementary School, Wolfville, NS

Antigonish County

    Denise Delorey, Save Community Schools, Heatherton, NS.

    Randy Delorey, H.J. MacDonald School, Heatherton, NS

Cape Breton Region

    Kate Oland, Middle River School, Victoria County, NS

    Pam Marson-Berk, *Middle River School, Victoria County, NS*

    Gerri Samson, West Richmond Education Centre, Evanston, NS

Digby County

    Jamie Lewis, Weymouth Consolidated School, Weymouth, NS

    Larry Donald Haight, Weymouth Board of Trade, Weymouth, NS

Halifax Regional Municipality

    Paul W. Bennett, Schoolhouse Consulting, Halifax

    Sandra Labor, Shatford Memorial Elementary School, Hubbards, NS

    Gordon Tate, Shatford Memorial Elementary School, Hubbards, NS

South Shore Region

    Michelle Wamboldt, Petite Riviere Elementary School

    Jens Laursen, Riverport School, Riverport

    Leif Helmer, Petite Riviere Elementary School

    Alastair Jarvis, HB Studios, Bridgewater

    Ron Stockton, Lunenburg Academy

    Barry Olivella, Lunenburg Academy

    Sherry Doucet, Pentz Elementary School, LeHave, NS

Appendix B

Legal Review — The School Review Process

Ron Stockton

The school review process is described in the *Education Act* and in the accompanying *Ministerial Education Act Regulations*.

There are two types of regulations:

1. *Ministerial regulations:* made by the Minister responsible for the *Act*, sometimes in consultation with other bodies.

2. *Governor in Council:* made by the Cabinet.

Both types of regulations are in place with respect to the *Education Act* and each has a prescribed jurisdiction. Ministerial regulations are made pursuant to the jurisdiction provided by s.145 of the *Act* while the Cabinet makes regulations pursuant to jurisdiction provided by s.146 of the *Act*. These distinctions are important to understand for the purposes of understanding school review and the ability of the provincial government to have some control over its spending on schools buildings (especially capital spending) and its ability to control spending while providing an appropriate education for the children of Nova Scotia.

The government of the province, during the losing struggle to save community schools on the south shore of the province in 2008-2009, repeatedly said that it did not have authority to intervene in the decision of a school board to close a school. This mantra was repeated by two PC and one NDP Ministers of Education. S.145(1)(n) of the *Act* gives the Minister authority to make regulations "*prescribing the decisions that may be made by a school board following a review of public schools.*" Ministerial regulation s.20(3), made under authority of s.145(1)(n) of the *Act*, provides that, "*[a] decision of a school board made in accordance with these regulations is final and shall not be altered by the Minister.*"

It can be seen then that the Minister made a regulation prohibiting her intervention and when asked to intervene relied on the prohibition to avoid intervention with a bad, and expensive, decision. In fact, the Minister, under authority of s.145(1)(n) of the *Act*, could simply have amended or repealed s.20(3) of the regulations and acted to preserve the community schools and save the provincial government millions of dollars.

This is but one illustration of the power the provincial government really has over school boards should it choose to take responsibility for the education system. Indeed, the province has absolute control, *"respecting the construction, location and control of public school buildings"* [s.146(1)(d) of the *Act*] through the regulations made by the Cabinet. Thus, even if the Minister could not alter a school board decision, there is no requirement that the province fund a new building or renovations of existing buildings to accommodate the students from the closed school.

S.89 of the *Act* permits a school board to identify a school for review [s.89(1)] and then requires that an identification of a school for review must be in accordance with the regulations [s.89(2)]. This section goes on to require a report to the public [s.89(3)], the formation of a study committee [s.89(4)], the publication of the study committee response [s.89(5)(a)] and the holding of a public meeting [s.89(5)(b)].

S.89A then provides the options for a school board after having followed the procedure in s.89. The options are: *status quo* [s.89A(a)], consolidate the school or part of it with another school [s.89A(b)], permanently close the school [s.89A(c)], or make any other decision authorized by the regulations [s.89A(d)].

As noted above, s.145 of the *Act* then gives the Minister the power to make regulations regarding the powers granted to the school board under s.89 and s.89A of the *Act*. Ministerial regulations 15 through 21 provide the details by which a school can be identified by a school board and the process that must be followed in order for the school board to make a decision.

Identification Report

Of particular note is s.16 of the regulations which deals with the Identification Report on each school to be reviewed that must be prepared by the school board before the school board can begin to review the school. This report must contain at least the following information:

- Enrollment patterns within the school region for the current and past five fiscal years [s.16(1)(a)]. The term "school region" is defined at s.3(1)(ag) of the *Act* as meaning *"the area over which a regional school board … exercises jurisdiction."* Thus, it appears that even if reviewing only one school the Identification Report must contain enrollment data for the whole of the school board's jurisdiction.
- Enrollment projections within the school region for the next five fiscal years [s.16(1)(b)]. This, it would seem, would require the school board to be working with demographers and development officers from both the province and the municipalities in the school board region.
- General population patterns and projections within the school region

for the past, current and next five fiscal year periods [s.16(1)(c)]. Again, it would be necessary to work closely with provincial and municipal demographers and development officers.
- Factors relating to the physical condition of the school(s) to be reviewed [s.16(1)(d)], including: (i) ability as a facility to deliver the program, (ii) facility utilization including excess space, (iii) condition of the building and its systems, (iv) costs associated with maintenance and operation.

The Identification Report then may contain information about any of the following [s.16(2)]:

- Current municipal or provincial plans for infrastructure development within the school region [s.16(2)(a)],
- Geographic isolation of the school [s.16(2)(b)],
- Factors related to student transportation to and from the school [s.16(2)(c)],
- Proposed development, including residential or economic, within the school region [s.16(2)(d)].

This information that "may" be included in the Identification Report is critical to accurately responding to the requirement of s.16(1)(b) and (c) of the regulations. Thus, to say the report "may" include the information seems absurd.

The Identification Report must be made available to the public by April 30th of the year in which the school board indicates the school will be reviewed [s.16(4)].

Impact Assessment Report

An Impact Assessment Report (IAR) must be prepared and made public by September 30th of the year in which the school board indicates a school will be reviewed [s.17(1)]. S.17(2) of the Ministerial regulations then sets out what must be contained in the Impact Assessment Report. In addition to matters related to the delivery of programs, staffing and property that must be provided, the IAR must contain information related to:

- The time and distance involved in transporting students to another school [s.17(2)(c)(iii)]. It would be interesting to see if the school board tends to underestimate the travel time.
- The ability of students to have access to extra-curricular activities if they are moved to a new school [s.17(2)(c)(iv)].
- The extent of community usage of the school to be closed over the last year [s.17(2)(c)(x)].

- Alternatives available to the community if the school closes [s.17(2)(c)(xi)].
- Any other impact on the community [s.17(2)(c)(xii)]. It is in this area in particular that the school board on the south shore failed to meet the criteria. It's only comment was that there would be a bit more traffic in the morning and afternoon. There was no attempt to review the economic or cultural impact on the community.

Study Committee

Once the IAR has been tabled, the school board must establish a Study Committee no later than October 7th of the year in which the school board indicates a school will be reviewed [s.18(1)]. The Study Committee will consist of the School Advisory Council for the school under review (except for student representatives) [s.18(2)] unless no SAC exists in which case a Study Committee of 5 to 16 people, selected from distinct groups, shall be created [s.18(3)]. This committee shall hold its first meeting no later than October 21st in the year the school review is announced.

The Study Committee shall prepare a response to the IAR and submit that response to the school board no later than February 1st of the year following the year during which the school review was initiated [s.18(12)], only after having held at least one public meeting [s.18(13)] and the report must contain a recommendation about the school board's decision to close a school [s.18(14)].

One notes that this Study Committee process takes place between October 7th and February 1st of the following year, that the Study Committee is made up mostly of volunteers from the community who, in many cases, would have work and family to look after and may have no experience at this kind of review, possibly leaving effective control in the hands of the Principal who is a member of the committee and that the work of the committee takes place over the Christmas season, effectively reducing the time available.

Public Hearing

Upon receipt of the Study Committee's response to the IAR, the school board shall table the response at a public meeting of the board, no later than February 28th [s.19(1)(a)] and make copies available to the public [s.19(1)(b)].

The school board shall then hold at least one public meeting, no later than March 24th of the year following the year in which the review is initiated, to allow representations from the public with respect to the IAR and the Study Committee response [s.19(2)].

Decision

No later than March 31st of the year following the year in which the review was initiated but after the public hearing noted above, the school board shall make its decision with respect to the outcome of the school review at a public meeting [s.20(1)] and shall post that decision within 15 days on the school board web site [s.20(2)].

The Minister may not alter the decision of the school board [s.20(3)] and if the decision is to close the school then it must permanently close the school within five years of the date of the decision [s.20(4)].

(Ron Stockton — March 2012)

"Sunday Drive Hangover": Transportation and Rural Community Life

A submission to the Atlantic Canada Regional Panel, SSHRC, University of New Brunswick, August 1, 2012. <http://atlanticregionalpanel.wordpress.com/>

By Kate Oland

When I was a child growing up in a small town in Nova Scotia, Sunday drives were a family ritual. My mom, dad, two brothers and I would pile into the station wagon, loaded down with tuna sandwiches and a Thermos of Kool-aid, and head out for a drive in the country. We explored every back road, nook, and cranny of Nova Scotia, marveling at the beauty and diversity of landscapes in our relatively small province.

Today, I have three children of my own, and I'm fortunate enough to live in rural Victoria County, Cape Breton. I think my kids are having a pretty good life, surrounded by natural wonders, in touch with the cycles of life and death on our mixed, subsistence farm, nurtured by their small, rural school, and engaged in their community.

But the Sunday drive is NOT a part of our family's tradition. Although I feel nostalgic about those family adventures, there are good reasons why we've dropped the Sunday drive ritual.

In my family (as in most rural families), driving is a necessity. We drive to town for work. We drive to town to buy the food we can't grow for ourselves. Our children ride the school bus for about an hour each day. We drive to visit friends, attend social activities, and take lessons. By Sunday, it's a luxury just to stay at home!

And on the rare occasions when we do take the children on a road trip, it's a decision we don't make lightly. Gasoline has become too expensive to waste on tooling around aimlessly, and the deplorable state of many rural roads means inevitable wear and tear on our trusty little car.

We've also grown more aware of the environmental impact of driving. Motoring merrily through the countryside loses some of its appeal when you think of it in terms of carbon emissions and climate change.

But while our family has jettisoned the "Sunday Drive mentality" which originated in a time of cheap gasoline, consumer exuberance, and environmental innocence, it seems the larger society is slower to change course. And for people living in rural areas, this happy motoring hangover is having serious consequences.

In an age of computer connectivity, higher gasoline prices, and heightened environmental sensitivity, it is frustrating that rural dwellers are still governed by the cheap oil mantras of "bigger is better" and "centralize for efficiency." Government services are largely centralized in urban areas, as are medical specialists. Perhaps most appallingly, rural schools continue to be threatened with closure, putting more rural children on longer bus rides to large schools far from home.

What does this mean "on the ground?" In Victoria County, Cape Breton, it means that if you want to obtain a GED, participate in adult or continuing education through the school board, meet with a business counselor, have a baby in the hospital, access employment counseling, attend a college or university course (unless you're participating in a course on a first nation reserve), or access most frontline mental health services (other than limited child and adolescent counseling services), you must leave the county. And you must leave it under your own steam, because there is no public transportation.

That means that a single parent hoping to complete a GED or attend adult high school, for example, must have access to a car, and must have the money to drive that car for about two hours a day to attend a course in the city.

It means that a family in which a parent is profoundly depressed and unable to work must somehow manage to find the gas money and emotional energy to travel to and from the city for psychiatric assistance or counseling. Follow-up care or support for the caregivers may also require trips to the city, as many specialists will not provide assistance by phone.

And it means that rural communities must fight, every few years, to prevent their dynamic, high-achieving, and beloved rural schools from closing. Communities know instinctively that new families will not move in if their children will have to ride the bus for two hours a day to reach the nearest school. What's at stake, for the children, is the erosion of educational quality, the loss of personal and family time, and the internalized message that they can't get what they need in their home community.

And the upshot of all of this? Poor literacy levels, unhealthy coping strategies (alcohol and drug use), a low rate of business startups, high levels of stress in communities, financial strain, and — of course — youth leaving for greener pastures.

It doesn't have to be this way. There are, in fact, some innovative service delivery methods that have the potential to make rural life less of a road trip.

Some of these models are in place already, but others will require community and political will to become reality.

Some examples of effective rural health delivery come to mind. There's the Nova Scotia Telehealth Network, a video conferencing communications network that connects healthcare facilities around Nova. Although the system is not yet being used to its full potential in every community, there are success stories. At the Inverness Hospital, for example, (one county over from Victoria County), people dealing with mental health issues attend an initial, in-office visit with a psychiatrist in the city, and then attend subsequent sessions from their community hospital via Telehealth — greatly reducing travel costs, costs in lost time and productivity, and patient stress.

There's also the Nova Scotia Breast Screening Program which, in addition to providing mammography at fixed locations across the province, operates three mobile mammography vehicles which take breast screening to rural communities. In 2008–2009, the Eastern mobile screening unit partnered with the Cape Breton District Health Authority and Cancer Care Nova Scotia to deliver a pilot "one stop cancer prevention clinic" to under serviced women in Cape Breton. The experience included a mammogram, a Pap test, a clinical breast examination, colon cancer screening education and a skin cancer assessment, as well as nutrition education for cancer prevention with a registered dietician. More than one thousand women attended one of 135 stop clinics in nine communities across Cape Breton. As one of the women who attended, I hope this pilot becomes a standard model of care. Instead of having to schedule five separate appointments, most of which would have required me to drive to the city, I was able to drop by the mobile unit at my community hospital and have everything completed there in under an hour.

The Strongest Families Institute is another rural health delivery success story. A not-for-profit company, Strongest Families offers home-based programs with telephone support to address childhood issues including difficult behavior, anxiety, recurring headache or abdominal pain, and bedwetting. Tested over a six-year period in the Centre for Research in Family Health at the IWK Health Centre in Halifax, the programs are offered to families free of charge and include workbooks, DVDs, and weekly phone meetings with Strongest Families coaches. Families learn and are supported in their own homes, at times convenient to them — and at no cost in terms of gas or lost productivity. The program has been so successful that Nova Scotia has just announced expansion of the service under its new Mental Health and Addictions strategy.

Outside the Health Sector, rural service delivery success stories become harder to find. As an employee of the Cape Breton Regional Library, I have to give a shout out to the Victoria County and Cape Breton County Bookmobiles — two of only a few bookmobiles still in operation in Nova

Scotia. Bookmobiles work hand in hand with online library software, making it possible for remote rural dwellers to order materials from any library in the region, for pickup at stops in their own communities. Bookmobiles work with schools, preschools, seniors' facilities, and community groups, and use innovative partnerships to deliver information and programs about healthy eating, physical fitness, and wise energy use, among other things.

Sadly, innovate service delivery development seems to be lagging in the field of education. In an era of declining student enrollment and funding cutbacks, school boards are under pressure to economize — and rural schools continue to be easy targets. There are goodwill gestures from the Department of Education, which talks a good game about supporting rural communities. The Department is working to improve online education (with plans to increase the number of students who can access online learning from 500 to 1500), it has tried to create a partnership-based service delivery model with its Schools Plus Program, and it continues to provide supplementary funding that's meant to allow boards to keep rural schools running.

Functionally, however, none of these initiatives go far enough. Isolated Small Schools funding, for example, is given to the boards for each isolated small school within its boundaries — but the money is in no way tied to the funded schools. Middle River School, for example, nets the school board $150,000 per year from the Province — a grant which almost completely covers the cost of running the school — but the guaranteed funding does not prevent the school board from repeatedly reviewing the school for closure. The argument, from the board's perspective, is that the "cost per square foot per student" is too high — even though the total cost of running the school is covered.

Similarly, online and distance learning — still very much in its infancy in this province — is not meeting the needs of most rural students. Teachers report that the current model only works well for highly motivated, independent learners. And, compared to the plethora of course offerings available in urban high schools, online course offerings remain meager.

The problem, as I see it, is the happy motoring hangover I referred to earlier. As a society, our "default setting" seems to favour closing rural schools and busing students to larger facilities far from home.

And this is particularly galling to me, as a rural parent, because the decision makers have not spent sufficient time on understanding the impact of busing. Although research in this area is sparse, there have been a few notable studies which looked at the effects of long bus rides on young children. These studies indicated that long bus rides reduced children's opportunities for physical activity and participation in extracurricular programs; decreased the amount of free time children had for homework, play, and family; affected their nutrition (as many were unable to stomach breakfast before a long, bumpy ride to school); affected what kinds of courses they took in high school (students on long bus rides knew they wouldn't have time to devote to more challenging course work); and reduced the likelihood of high school graduation.

Long bus rides are also a huge grey area in terms of bullying. In contrast to the school and the school yard, where student behavior is monitored and programs are in place to prevent bullying, the school bus is a no man's land. Bus drivers (quite rightly) need to keep their eyes on the road, and are not there primarily to supervise behavior. In rural settings, children as young as four may be on the bus with eighteen-year-olds. There are numerous anecdotal reports of inappropriate language, teasing, bullying, shoving, and inappropriate touching.

And the old argument — that children must endure these hours on the bus because they will be going to a "bigger, better" school — is hogwash. Decades of solid academic research confirms the educational advantages of small, community schools and multi-age classrooms. Children nurtured in small, community schools close to home in their formative years score higher on many social measures (cooperation, for example) than children in large, centralized schools. They also benefit from an educational setting which includes — and is the heart of — their community; where community members volunteer in the classroom and participate actively in the life of the school.

We need to see the kind of innovation that is becoming apparent in health care applied to public education in the rural setting, if we are going to keep rural children in their home communities and "off the road." What might this look like? Here's a short list:

- Start by embracing the idea that schools should be at the center of every community, and that those schools should be centers of lifelong learning for all citizens.

- Make use of existing technology to support rural classroom learning. Link small, isolated schools with other schools to exchange ideas or share teaching time.

- Listen to rural voices and consider returning to a rural-centered curriculum that would encourage children to think creatively and entrepreneurially about living in rural areas.

- In literacy-poor counties like Victoria, create a Continuing Education Facilitator position. If community schools were community learning centers equipped with appropriate technology, the Facilitator could help adults obtain a GED, access distance and online learning from community colleges and universities, lead online meetings with community groups from across the region, and help people learn computer and technology skills.

- Seriously beef up distance learning opportunities for rural high school students, and look at delivery models including small group learning linked to an actual teacher and classroom elsewhere.
- Consider whether charter schools might be an option, if the political will to support public rural learning does not manifest.
- Consider whether meaningful supports to home schooling families might be an option, if the political will to support public rural learning does not manifest.

Appendix D

Pathway to Rural Regeneration

Brief of the Nova Scotia Small Schools Initiative to the Nova Scotia Commission on the New Economy, April 2013

Key Recommendations

We call upon the Nova Scotia Commission on the New Economy to take the lead in addressing the looming crisis affecting rural and small town Nova Scotia, driven by worrisome rural depopulation trends and aggravated by the recurrent cycles of small school closures and their potentially devastating consequences for what remains of rural life.

The Nova Scotia Small School Initiative, composed of parent and community activists from all parts of Nova Scotia, recommends a province-wide strategy seeking to arrest the disturbing trend and to provide rural communities with a reason for hope in the 21st century.

It is recommended that:

1. The Nova Scotia Commission take the lead by embracing a *Community School at the Centre* philosophy aimed at revitalizing rural communities through a province-wide, community-building and development strategy focusing on rehabilitating neglected school communities. Instead of abandoning small schools to a School Review for closure process, move schools to the centre of planning for the future.

2. The Commission support a Moratorium on the School Review process, covering all schools identified in the current provincial cycle of school accommodation reviews. Such a move would send a powerful signal that the current School Review process is broken, acknowledging that it's adversarial, divisive, destroys confidence in the public system —and needs to be re-examined as a go-forward strategy.

3. The Commission recommend to the Premier the adoption of a Rural Revitalization Strategy, working with five different departments, Education, Economic and Rural Development, Health, Community Services, and Cultural Affairs/Libraries, and generated though a public engagement process involving all interested

groups, including school boards, regional development agencies, school councils, teachers, local boards of trade, local government and citizens.

4. A Rural Education and Development Strategy take precedence over a School Review process in charting the future of rural and small town Nova Scotia. Consider a one-year moratorium on school closures to provide a "time-out" and focus our energies on exploring and developing community-based alternative approaches.

5. The Commission consider the advantages of recommending a Public Engagement Model in place of the current quasi-judicial School Review process seeking to find community-based solutions and rendering most, if not all, School Reviews unnecessary exercises. Such a Model could actually run in tandem with, and be fully integrated with, Community Development Plans.

6. A Ministerial Review be initiated fully examining the Education Act and Regulations as they relate to school reviews, with a view to levelling the playing field by shifting the *burden of proof* to those seeking school shutdowns. Instead of simply bolstering School Review Committees, raise the bar for school boards so that the process is reserved as a strategy of last resort.

7. Build on the *Nova Scotia Virtual School* project by initiating a Rural Schools Online Education Network, based upon the Newfoundland model, creating digitally-networked schools and taking fuller advantage of distance education in the 21st century guise of virtual schooling. Seek amendments to the Education Act and the collective agreements to remove obstacles to providing blended online and regular learning programs in rural and remote parts of the province.

8. The Commission embrace a Social Sustainability Framework and examine carefully the innovative community planning ventures recommended by the Young Foundation in the United Kingdom and now being implemented in a number of municipalities in Alberta and British Columbia. Generate a Rural Strategy, based upon Social Sustainability principles, resting on the fundamental pillars of Schools at the Centre, Community Partnerships, ICT Innovation, and Sustainable Economic and Social Development.

9. The Commission take the lead in proposing a Community Hub School model as the centrepiece of a province-wide strategy aimed at promoting rural regeneration, community-led innovation, and the long—term sustainability of our threatened rural communities.

Nova Scotia Small Schools Initiative, Core Supporters, March 2013

Annapolis Valley Region
- Michael Corbett, School of Education, Acadia University
- Steven Rhude, Wolfville Elementary School, Wolfville, NS
- Debbie Francis, Newport Station Elementary School, Newport Station, NS

Antigonish County
- Denise Delorey, Save Community Schools, Heatherton, NS.
- Randy Delorey, Save Community Schools, Heatherton, NS

Cape Breton
- Kate Oland, Middle River School, Victoria County, NS
- Pam Marson-Berk, Middle River School, Victoria County, NS
- Gerri Samson, West Richmond Education Centre, Evanston, NS

Colchester County
- Anita MacLellan, Upper Economy, NS
- Tory Phinney, Bass River Elementary School, Bass River NS
- Tanya Harnish, Bass River Elementary School
- Maurice Rees, *The Shoreline Journal*, Bass River, NS

Cumberland County
- Cecil McLeod, Wentworth Consolidated School, Wentworth, NS
- Carol Hislop, Wentworth Consolidated School

Digby County
- Jamie Lewis, Weymouth Consolidated School, Weymouth, NS
- Larry Donald Haight, Weymouth Board of Trade, Weymouth, NS

East Hants County
- Cathrine Yuill, Maitland Consolidated School, Maitland, NS
- Kevin Quinlan, Principal, NSCC Truro
- Kim Henwood, Maitland Consolidated School, Maitland, NS

Halifax Regional Municipality
- Paul W. Bennett, Schoolhouse Consulting
- Sandra Labor, Shatford Memorial Elementary School, Hubbards, NS
- Gordon Tate, Shatford Memorial Elementary School, Hubbards, NS
- Matt d'Entremont, Lower Sackville, NS

Lunenburg County
- Leif Helmer, NSCC Bridgewater, Petite Riviere, NS
- Michelle Wamboldt, Petite Riviere Elementary School

- Jens Laursen, Riverport School, Riverport
- Ron Stockton, Lunenburg Academy
- Barry Olivella, Lunenburg Academy
- Sherry Doucet, Pentz Elementary School, LeHave, NS
- Christopher Gill, Petite Riviere, NS

Pictou County
- Abby Taylor, River John Consolidated School
- Rob Assels, FLAWed Productions, River John, NS
- Dan Ferguson, Simpsons Appliances and Repairs, River John, NS
- Rev. Greg Dickson, St. George's Presbyterian Church, River John, NS
- Monica Graham, Freelance Writer, Sundridge, Pictou County
- Sheree Fitch, Author, River John, NS

Queen's County
- Jessica Van Dyne-Evans, Mill Village Consolidated School, Mill Village, NS
- Catherine Croft, Mill Village Consolidated School, Mill Village, NS
- Terry Rafuse, Gold River Western Shore School
- Sarah Swinamer, Gold River Western Shore School

Yarmouth County
- Janessa Blauvelt, Arcadia Consolidated School, Yarmouth
- John Levac, Arcadia Consolidated School, Yarmouth
- Debra Saulnier, Arcadia Consolidated School, Yarmouth

News Release — Nova Scotia Education Minister Requests Halt to School Closure Process, 3 April, 2013*

The province launched a course of action today, April 3, to ensure the school-review process is fairer and better reflects the interests of students and communities.

Education and Early Childhood Development Minister Ramona Jennex wrote school boards to request the school-review process for 2013–14 be suspended while a new review process is being developed. She also asked the boards to delay any school closings decided in 2012–13 until the new process is in place.

The interim report from the Commission on Building Our New Economy, expected this fall, will also be used in developing the new approach.

"Schools are the heart of a community and community schools have been an important focus for this government," said Ms. Jennex. "We are hearing from parents and families that recent changes to the school-review process didn't go far enough, so we need to develop a more collaborative process on how we deal with community schools and school-reviews.

The Kids and Learning First plan places an emphasis on community schools. The Schools Plus initiative puts government services for youth, families and seniors in schools and community use of grants allow people to use the schools for free or at a low cost. The province also supports small, isolated schools with additional funding to help keep them open.

"This wasn't an easy decision to make, but it is the right decision," said Ms. Jennex. "As the minister, I had to reach out to boards to ensure the process is stopped until further changes take place. We've listened to parents, school boards, communities and municipalities who have told us this process needs a major overhaul."

The Commission on Building Our New Economy, headed by Ray Ivany, is looking at how provincial priorities of innovation, skills training and competitiveness work in a local context, in tourism, manufacturing and primary production sectors, for young people, workers and families that seek a better life in their home communities.

"We will invite school boards, communities and other stakeholders to help in developing a new school-review process," Ms. Jennex said.

The review will also include the current process of turning schools over to municipalities after they are closed.

A discussion paper for public input will be ready this fall and the new process is expected to be in place by spring 2014.

News Release: "New School Review Process to be Developed," Education and Early Childhood Development, April 3, 2013 1:09 PM

References

Antigonish *Casket.* 2010. "Never Assume." Editorial, 26 October.

AVRSB (Annapolis Valley Regional School Board). 2010. *Charting a Course for the Future: Education Delivery in the Annapolis Valley School Board.* Berwick, NS: AVRSB, April.

____. 2011. *Successful Schools for Successful Students.* Berwick, NS: AVRSB, October 5.

Barley, Z., and A. Beesley. 2007. "Rural School Success: What Can We Learn?" *Journal of Research in Rural Education* 22, 1.

Beaumont, Constance E., and Elizabeth G. Pianca. 2002. *Why Johnny Can't Walk to School: Historic Neighborhoods in the Age of Sprawl.* Washington, DC: National Trust for Heritage Preservation.

Bell, D., and M. Jayne. 2010. "The Creative Countryside: Policy and Practice in the UK Rural Cultural Economy." *Journal of Rural Studies* 26, 3: 209–18.

Bennett, Paul W. 2011. *Vanishing Schools, Threatened Communities: The Contested Schoolhouse in Maritime Canada, 1850–2010.* Halifax: Fernwood Publishing.

____. 2013a. *Pathway to Rural Regeneration: Transforming Small Schools into Community Hubs.* Brief to the Nova Scotia Commission on the New Economy. Halifax: NSSSI, April.

____. 2013b. "Reclaiming At-Risk Children and Youth: A Review of Nova Scotia's *SchoolsPlus* Program." Halifax: AIMS Research Report, June.

Bennett, Paul W., et al. 2012. "Stop the Ticking Clock in Rural N.S." *Chronicle Herald,* 19 May.

Beswick, Aaron. 2012a. "Strait Votes to Close Heatherton School." 6 March.

____. 2012b. "Parents Suing Strait School Board." 26 May.

____. 2012c. "School Lets Out on High Note." 23 June.

Boon, Helen J. 2011. "Beliefs and Education for Sustainability in Rural and Regional Australia." *Education in Rural Australia* 1 July: 1–11.

Boone, Wilbert. 2007. *The Evolution of E-Learning in Small Rural Schools in Newfoundland and Labrador.* Research paper. Killick Centre for E-Learning Research, Faculty of Education, Memorial University of Newfoundland.

Brighton, Rachel. 2013. "Let's Keep Doors Open at Schools." *Sunday Herald,* 24 March.

British Columbia Teachers' Federation. 2008. "Issues in Education: School Closures, Report to MLAs." April 9; and "Background Information." <http://bctf.ca/IssuesInEducation>.

Canadian Council on Learning. 2006. *The Rural-Urban Gap in Education.* Ottawa: CCL, March.

Canmac Economics. 2012a. *Nova Scotia Regions Demographic Outlook.* Research report for Union of Nova Scotia Municipalities.

____. 2012b. *Economic Outlook.* Research report for Union of Nova Scotia Municipalities, 5 November.

Castells, Manuel. 2004. *The Power of Identity: Vol. 2, The Information Society: Economy, Society, and Culture.* Malden, MA: Blackwell.

CBC News. 2013. "Maritime Economy in Deep Trouble, Expert Warns." CBC Radio News, Nova Scotia, 5 February.

CBC Television. 2009. "Rural Schools." *Land and Sea* series, hosted by Tom Murphy, 13 September.

Chronicle Herald. 2012a. "New Model Schooling." Editorial, 17 April.

____. 2012b. "New Model Schooling: The Heart of a Revival." Editorial, 27 May.

____. 2012c. "Old Schools for New: $100-Million Opportunity." Editorial, 28 November.

___. 2012d. "Economic Development: Rural Restart." Editorial, 30 November.

____. 2013a. "Small School Closures: Think Bigger." Editorial. 29 March: A7.

___. 2013b. "New Model Schools: From Hubbub to Local Hubs." Editorial, 4 April.

CCN (Coastal Communities Network). 2013. "About Us." <http://www.coastalcommunities.ns.ca/>.

Clandfield, David. 2010. "The School as a Community Hub: A Public Alternative to the Neo-Liberal Threat to Ontario Schools." *Our Schools Our Selves* 19, 1: 5–74.

Colantonio, A., and T. Dixon. 2009. *Managing Socially Sustainable Urban Regeneration in Europe.* Oxford Brookes University: Oxford Institute for Sustainable Development (OISD).

Comeau, Tina. 2013a. "Make Schools the Hubs of Communities." *Yarmouth Vanguard*, 19 March: 29

___. 2013b. "Hub School Concept Gaining Momentum." *Yarmouth Vanguard*, 5 April.

___. 2011. "Pitches Made to Save Weymouth School." *Digby Courier*, 7 December.

Community Schools Alliance. 2009. "Announcement Message from Southwest Middlesex Mayor Doug Reycraft, Middlesex, Ontario." 17 August. <www.CommunitySchoolsAlliance.ca>.

Conference Board of Canada. 1992. *Employment Skills Profile: The Critical Skills Required of the Canadian Workforce.* Ottawa: Conference Board of Canada.

Conrad, Dee, and Leif Helmer. 2013. *Our Vision for the Petite Riviere Community School: A Response to the Impact Assessment Report.* Petite Riviere, NS: PRES Study Committee, 31 January.

Corbett, Michael. 2004. "It Was Fine, If You Wanted to Leave: Narratives of Educational Ambivalence from a Nova Scotia Coastal Community 1963–1998. *Anthropology and Education Quarterly* 35: 451–71.

___. 2006. "Educating the Country Out of the Child and the Child Out of the Country: An Excursion in Spectrology." *Alberta Journal of Educational Research* 52, 4 (Winter): 289–301.

___. 2007a. *Learning to Leave: The Irony of Schooling in a Rural Coastal Community.* Halifax: Fernwood Publishing.

___. 2007b. "Travels in Space and Place: Identity and Rural Schooling." *Canadian Journal of Education* 3, 3: 771–92. <www.mikecorbett.ca/files/PDF/latest/CJE30-3-2007Corbett.pdf>.

___. 2010. "Answering My Sister's Question: The Critical Importance of Education for Diversity in Those Spaces Where We Think We Are all the Same." *Journal of Inquiry and Action in Education* 3, 3.

___. 2012. "The Magic Bus and Rural Education." Address to the Small Schools Summit, 21 January, NSCC, Bridgewater, NS.

Corbett, Michael, and Dennis Mulcahy. 2006. *Education on a Human Scale: Small Rural Schools in a Modern Context.* Municipality of Cumberland County, Research Report 061. Wolfville, NS: Acadia University Centre for Rural Education.

Corbett, Michael, and Ann Vibert. 2010. "Curriculum as a Safe Place: Parental Perceptions of New Literacies in a Rural Small Town School." *Canadian Journal of Educational Administration and Policy* 114, 2 December.

Cotton, K. 1996. "School Size, School Climate, and Student Performance." *School Improvement Research Studies.*

Courchene, Thomas. 1970. "Inter-Provincial Migration and Economic Adjustment." *Canadian Journal of Economics* 3: 550–76.

Dare, Malkin, and Paul W. Bennett. 2011. Don't Shutter Small Schools, Open Them Up to Community." *Chronicle Herald*, 17 December.

Delaney, Gordon. 2012. "Valley Board to Close Two Schools." *Chronicle Herald*, 21 March.

Deloitte. 2012. "The Future of Productivity: An Eight-Step Game Plan for Canada." Presentation to Greater Halifax Partnership Conference, Halifax, NS, 24 May.

Delorey, Denise, et al. 2012. "Rev. H.J. Macdonald Study Committee Response to SRSB Impact Assessment Report." Heatherton, NS, 31 January.

Ecology Action Centre. 2011. "Active and Safe Routes to School." Brochure, Ecology Action Centre and Health Promotion and Protection, Government of Nova Scotia.

Egan, John. 2004. *The Egan Review: Skills for Sustainable Communities*. Office of the Deputy Prime Minister, London: OPDM.

Elliott, Joy. 2005. *Researching Healthy and Sustainable Development in Nova Scotia*. Halifax: Atlantic Health Promotion Research Centre, Coastal Communities Network, and Dalhousie University, December.

Elliott, Patricia W. 2011. "School Consolidation and Notions of Progress." University of Regina, Regina. SK. <www.ineducation.ca>.

Fox, Michael. 1996. "Rural Transportation as a Daily Constraint in Students' Lives." *Rural Educator.*

Funk, Patricia E., and Jon Bailey. 1999. "Small Schools, Big Results: Nebraska High School Completion and Postsecondary Enrollment Rates by Size of School District." Nebraska Alliance for Rural Education, Research Report (September).

Gill, Chris. 2012a. "Consider Community Factor When Closing Small Schools." *Chronicle Herald,* 10 March.

_____. 2012b. "A Message to You Quaint Rural Folk." *Lunenburg-Bridgewater Bulletin* 28 March.

Gorman, Michael. 2012. "Fear of Change Holding Back N.S., Pollster." *Chronicle Herald*, 28 June.

_____. 2013. "Schools on the Block." *Chronicle Herald*, 21 March.

Government of Alberta. 2005. *A Place to Grow Alberta's Rural Development Strategy.* Executive Summary. Edmonton, February.

Government of British Columbia. 2009. *Reversing the Tide: Strategies for Success Rural Revitalization Project.* Summary paper — Revitalizing Rural British Columbia: Some Lessons from Rural America. Victoria.

Government of Manitoba. 2002. *Rural Education in Manitoba: Defining Challenges, Creating Solutions.* Winnipeg.

Government of PEI. 2010. *Rural Action Plan: A Rural Economic Development Strategy for Prince Edward Island.* Charlottetown.

Graves, Diana. 2011. *Exploring Schools as Community Hubs.* Regina: Faculty of Arts Community Research Unit, University of Regina.

Greencorn, Troy. 2012. "Community Engagement Key to Rural Development." *Chronicle Herald,* 8 December.

Gülümser, A., T. Baycan-Levent, and P. Nijkamp. 2010. "Measuring Regional Creative Capacity: A Literature Review for Rural-Specific Approaches." *European Planning Studies* 18, 4: 545–63.

Gunn, James. 2007a. *The Relationship Between Learning and Grade Configuration and How it May Influence the Use of Schools in Nova Scotia.* Halifax: Department of Education and Gunn's Leadership Consulting Services, March.

_____. 2007b. *Optimal School Size.* Halifax: Department of Education and Gunn's Leadership Consulting Services, October.

Haight, Larry Donald. 2011. "Weymouth Board of Trade Presentation." Tri-County Regional School Board, 6 December.

Hamilton, Sylvia. 2007. *The Little Black Schoolhouse.* Documentary film.

Harris, C. 1998. *A Sense of Themselves: Elizabeth Murray's Leadership in School and Community.* Halifax: Fernwood.

Haynes, Kathryn Harley. 2013. "Meeting Design: Form and Function." *Progress Magazine* 20, 1: 41–44.

Helmer, Leif. 2013. "Why Small Schools Cost Less." *Bridgewater Bulletin*, 13 February.

Howley, Craig. 1996. "Compounding Disadvantage: The Effects of School and District Size on Student Achievement in West Virginia." *Journal of Research in Education.*

___. 1997. "How to Make Rural Education Research *Rural:* An Essay at Practical Advice." *Journal of Research in Rural Education* 13, 2: 131–38.

Howley, Craig, Aimee Howley, and Steven Shamblen. 2001. "Riding the School Bus: A Comparison of the Rural and Suburban Experience in Five States." *Journal of Research in Rural Education* 17, 1 (Spring): 41–63.

Huggins, R., and N. Clifton. 2011. "Competitiveness, Creativity, and Place-Based Development." *Environment and Planning* 43, 6: 1341–62.

Jackson, David. 2012a. "Parties Play Census Blame Game." *Chronicle Herald*, 9 February.

___. 2012b. "Tapping into Our Rural Roots." *Chronicle Herald*, 30 November.

Jeffrey, Davene. 2013. "Ivany Happy with Turnout for Economic Meeting." *Chronicle Herald*, 13 February.

Kelley, Lorry Anne (2013). "Letter to Families: New School vs..Renovation." *Newsletter,* Windsor Forks District School, 21 January 2013.

Kelly, Nancy. 2011. "Forgotten School." Kings County *Register,* 6 December.

___. 2012a. "Cambridge Parents Want School to Survive." 9 January.

___. 2012b. "Closing Cambridge School 'Unacceptable': Toney." 14 March.

___. 2012c. "Hope for a New Cambridge School." 11 April.

Kuhlman, Renee. 2010. *Helping Johnny Walk to School.* Washington, DC: National Trust for Heritage Preservation, March.

Labor, Sandra, and Shatford Memorial Elementary School. 2009. *Rural Education: A School and Community Partnership.* Hubbards, NS: SMES Rural Strategy Parent Focus Group, October.

Laursen, Jens, et al. 2011. "School Review Process." Parent group letter to Ramona Jennex, Minister of Education, 6 July.

Lawrence, Barbara Kent, et al. 2002. *Dollars & Sense: The Cost Effectiveness of Small Schools.* Cincinnati: Knowledge Works Foundation.

Leger, Dan. 2012. " Population Drain: Fewer Nova Scotians, More Problems." *Chronicle Herald*, 24 December.

___. 2013. "Want to Save Small Towns? Save Their Schools." *Chronicle Herald*, 4 February.

Lenihan, Don. 2012. *Rescuing Policy: The Case for Public Engagement.* Ottawa: Public Policy Forum.

Levin, Ben. 2011. *Steps to Effective and Sustainable Public Education in Nova Scotia.* Halifax: Nova Scotia Department of Education, April.

Lightstone, Michael. 2012. "Prepare for Rural Decline, Expert Says." *Chronicle Herald*, 6 November.

Lindsay, David. 2012. "Want to Save Small Rural Schools? Occupy!"; "It's About Equity." *Rural Delivery*, March: 18–25.

Lunenburg County Community Fund. 2010. *Lunenburg County Vital Signs.* <http://www. cfns.ca/pages/documents/LUNENBURGCOUNTYSVITALSIGNS2010.pdf>.

Lyson, Thomas A. 2002. "What Does a School Mean to a Community? Assessing the Social and Economic Benefits of Schools to Rural Villages in New York." *Journal of Research in Rural Education.*

MacDonald, Joyce. 2003. "The Process and Impact of School Closures in Four Rural Nova Scotian Communities." Halifax: Rural Communities Impacting Policy. <www.ruralnovascotia.com>.

MacDonald, Mary Jess. 2012. "Changes Urged for N.S. School Review Process." CBC News Nova Scotia, 9 March.

MacKenzie, Amy. 2013. "Rural Regeneration." *The News* (New Glasgow, NS): 1, 3.

McCann, P. (ed.). 1982. *Blackboards and Briefcases: Personal Stories by Newfoundland Teachers, Educators and Administrators.* St. John's, NL: Jesperson.

McNiven, Jim. 2006. *Summary of the Nova Scotia Demographic Research Report: A Demographic Analysis of Nova Scotia into 2026.* Halifax: Canmac Economics and Jozsa Management and Economics, December.

Medel, Brian. 2011. "Weymouth School on List for Possible Closure." *Chronicle Herald*, 31 October.

____. 2012. "Board Urged to Keep Weymouth School." *Chronicle Herald*, 10 March.

Mulcahy, Dennis. 1996. "Why Rural Education?" Academic paper, Faculty of Education, Memorial University of Newfoundland, Fall.

____. 2009. "Rural and Remote Schools: A Reality in Search of a Policy." Policy Paper, Edge Conference, October, St. John's, NL.

Nova Scotia. N.D. <www.gov.ns.ca/fina/communitycounts/>.

Nova Scotia Commission on the New Economy. 2013. "About the Economy of Nova Scotia." Information Sheet. Truro: OneNS.

Nova Scotia Education. 2009. "Discussion Notes, School Review Process Focus Group." December.

____. 2012. *Kids and Learning First.* Halifax: Department of Education, February.

Nova Scotia Education and Child Development. 2013. "New School Review Process to be Developed." News release, 3 April.

Nova Scotia Government. 2007. *Our Kids Are Worth It: Strategy for Children and Youth.* Halifax: Department of Community Services.

____. 2010. *Weaving the Threads: A Lasting Social Fabric — Our Framework for Social Prosperity.* Halifax: Government of Nova Scotia.

____. 2013. *Nova Scotia Community Counts.* Census for 2006 and 2011, Nova Scotia; Maitland; and Weymouth. 3 March.

NSDoE. 2006. "School Boards Asked to Hold Off School Reviews." News Release, March 29.

NSSBA (Nova Scotia School Boards Association). 2010. *A Call for Greater Interdepartmental Delivery of Services to Youth and Families in Nova Scotia.* Chair of project: Vic Fleury. Dartmouth: NSSBA Education Committee, March.

NSSSI (Nova Scotia Small Schools Initiative). 2012. *Schools at the Centre: A Revitalization Strategy for Rural Communities.* Brief to the Minister of Education. Halifax: NSSD, 15 May.

O'Brien, Catherine. 2008. "Sustainable Happiness and the Trip to School." *World Transport Policy & Practice* 14, 1: 15–26.

O'Brien, Catherine, and Richard Gilbert. 2010. *Guidelines for Child and Youth-Friendly Land-use and Transport Planning in Rural Areas.* <www.researchgate.net/publication/228715383_GUIDELINES_FOR_CHILD-AND_YOUTH-FRIENDLY_LAND-USE_AND_TRANSPORT_PLANNING_IN_RURAL_AREAS>.

Oland, Kate. 2012. "School Review Process Seriously Flawed." *Chronicle Herald*, 9 February.

Ontario Ministry of Municipal Affairs and Housing. 2004 and 2006. "Ontario's Rural Plan (2004 and 2006) Strong Rural Communities: Working Together for Success." Toronto. <www.ruralplan.ontario.ca>.

___. 2006. "Update 2006." Toronto. <www.ruralplan.ontario.ca>.

People for Education. 2008. "Declining Enrolment in Ontario Schools." *Annual Report on Ontario's Public Schools 2008*. <www.peopleforeducation.ca/document/declining-enrolment-2008/>.

___. 2009. "Accommodation Reviews 2009." <www.peopleforeducation.ca/document/accommodation-reviews-2009/>.

Pilkey, Dennis W. 2009. *Final Report — Rural Development Assessment*. Coastal Communities Network. Dartmouth: D.W. Pilkey Consulting, March.

Pitts, Gordon. 2012. "The Oracle of Oxford, N.S." *Globe and Mail*, 1 December: B3.

Pollett, Graham L. 2008. *The Impact of Bus Time on Child and Youth Health*. Middlesex-London Health Unit, Report 135-08, 16 October.

Putnam, Robert. 2001. *Bowling Alone: The Collapse and Revival of American Community*. New York: Touchstone Books.

Ramage, Rob, and Aimee Howley. 2005. "Parents' Perceptions of the Rural School Bus Ride." *Rural Educator* Fall: 15–25.

Raywid, Mary Anne. 1999. "Current Literature on Small Schools." Eric Digest.

RCIPP (Rural Communities Impacting Policy Project). 2003. *Painting the Landscape of Rural Nova Scotia*. New Glasgow, NS: Coastal Communities MNetwork and Atlantic Health Promotion Research Centre, Dalhousie University, October.

Rees, Maurice. 2013. "Are You Feeling Marginalized?" Rees's Pieces Column, *The Shoreline Journal* (Bass River, NS). March.

Riley, Jonathan. 2012. "Weymouth School Committee Gives Impact Assessment a Poor Grade." Digby County *Courier*, 13 January.

RIRDC (Rural Industries Research and Development Corporation). 2002. *More than an Education*. Hobart, Australia: University of Tasmania.

Sederberg, Charles H. 1987. "The Economic Role of School Districts in Rural Communities." *Journal of Research in Rural Education* 4, 3: 125–30.

Senate of Canada. 2008. *Beyond Freefall: Halting Rural Poverty*. Final report of the Standing Senate Committee on Agriculture and Forestry. Ottawa, June.

Sharpe, Errol. 1991. "From the Past to the Future: Rethinking Rural Society and Social Change." Unpublished M.A. thesis, Saint Mary's University.

Sher, Jonathan P. (ed.). 1978. *Rural Education in America: A Reassessment of the Conventrional Wisdom*. Boulder, CO: Westview Press.

Shiers, Kelly. 2012. "Committee Urges Province to Keep Rural Schools Open." *Chronicle Herald*, 17 May.

Small School Summit. 2012. *Agenda, Small School Summit 2012*. 21 January, NSCC Bridgewater.

Smitheram, Verner. 1982. "Development and the Debate over School Consolidation." In Verner Smitheram et al. (eds.), *The Garden Transformed: Prince Edward Island, 1945–1980*. Charlottetown: Ragweed Press.

Stephenson, Marilla. 2012. "Regional Economic Development Reform Would Be Welcome." *Chronicle Herald*, 29 November.

Stockton, Ron. 2012. *Legal Review of School Review Process*. Small Schools Delegation research paper, March.

Stolarick, K., M. Denstedt, B. Donald, and G. Spencer. 2010. "Creativity, Tourism and Economic Development in a Rural Context: The Case of Prince Edward County." *Journal of Rural and Community Development* 5, 1–2: 238–54.

Stone, Michael K. 2009. *Smart by Nature: Schooling for Sustainability*. Berkley: Watershed Media, University of California Press.

Sullivan, Keith, and Kathleen. 2011. "Education in Small Schools; Accentuate the Positive." *Chronicle Herald*, 22 December 2012.

Supreme Court of Nova Scotia. 2012. *Delorey v. Strait Regional School Board*, NSSC 227, Justice Patrick J. Murray. Heard 22 May. Decision, 4 January 2013.

Surette, Ralph. 2012. "Rural Development and Dexter's Jobs Obsession." *Chronicle Herald*, 1 December.

Sutherland, Mary Beth, and Abby Taylor. 2013. "The River John Community School Hub: A New Proposal for the Chignecto-Regional School Board." 28 February.

TCRSB (Tri-County Regional School Board). 2012. *Minutes of Special Board Meeting*. 27 March: 4–8.

Truscott, D.M., and S.D. Truscott. 2005. "Differing Circumstances, Shared Challenges: Finding Common Ground Between Urban and Rural Schools." *Phi Delta Kappa*.

Verges, Josh. 2011. "Four Rural S.D. Schools Let Students Run Show." *Argus Leader*, 23 July.

___. 2013. "Technology might save small schools." *Argus Leader*, 13 February.

Wallin, Dawn C. 2009. *Rural Education: A Review of Provincial and Territorial Initiatives*. Ottawa: Canadian Council on Learning and Government of Canada.

Ware, Beverley. 2011. "Education Minister Fires South Shore School Board." *Chronicle Herald*, 29 November.

___. 2012. "Castle on the Hill Closing." *Chronicle Herald*, 8 March.

___. 2013a. "South Shore Board Votes to Close Four Schools." *Chronicle Herald*, 28 March: A8.

___. 2013b. "Closed Schools Would Burden Taxpayers." *Chronicle Herald*, 2 April 2012.

Willick, Frances. 2013. "Schools Under Siege" series. *Chronicle Herald*, 25 March, 26 March, and 27 March.

Willick, Frances, and Michael Lightstone. 2012. "Empty Classrooms, Wasted Dollars." *Chronicle Herald*, 27 November.

Woodcraft, Saffron, Tricia Hackett, and Lucia Caistor-Arendar. 2012. *Design for Social Sustainability: A Framework for Creating Thriving New Communities*. London: The Young Foundation.

Index

aging population, of Nova Scotia 11, 12, 14, 17

"airport terminal" high schools 24

Annapolis Royal Academy, and its closure 57, 58

Annapolis Valley First Nation, on school closures 55

Annapolis Valley Regional School Board (AVRSB) 56, 62-63, 64, 67, 118

Arcadia Consolidated School, Yarmouth 95, 115

Austin, Mark 44

Bass River Elementary School, and closure battle 23, 31, 35, 76, 86, 114

Beaton, Jack (SRSB Superintendent) 69, 72, 73

Bennett, Paul W. 18, 24, 59, 67, 68, 70, 87, 100, 114, 118, 120

Beyond Freefall (Senate Committee Report, 2008) 1, 36, 40, 124

"big box" elementary schools 24, 34, 35, 54, 59, 84, 85, 94, 95-96

"bigger is better" mentality 83, 107

Blauvelt, Janessa viii, 95, 115

bookmobiles, and rural library service 108-109

Bluenose Academy, Lunenburg (see "big box" elementary schools)

Bragg, John, of Oxford Frozen Foods 9, 10

Broadband for Rural Nova Scotia (BRNS) 38

budget cuts, to education 2, 36, 44

bullying, on school buses 26, 28, 30, 67, 84, 110

Cambridge School (AVRSB) 57, 58, 121

Canso, and Stan Rogers Folk Festival 53

"central corridor," and NS demographic trend 1, 7, 11, 52, 76

centralized administration, and regionalization 1, 96, 97

Chignecto-Central Regional School Board (CCRSB) 18, 19, 22, 39, 75, 85-86, 94

Clandfield, David vii, 77- 79, 119

Coastal Communities Network, origins of 42-46, 119

Coastal Communities Network, research and advocacy 11, 13-15, 39, 40, 51, 84, 120, 123

collapse of ground fishery, in 1990s 42, 52

Comeau, Tina, of Yarmouth *Vanguard* 59, 92, 95, 119

Commission on Our New Economy (NS, 2013) 7, 9-11, 86, 116, 121

Community Counts, and rural communities 15, 43, 91, 123

community hub schools vii, 7, 40, 77-80, 87, 96, 119

Conrad, Dee, of Petite Riviere 84, 88

Corbett, Michael vii, 6, 7, 21, 27, 28, 30, 33, 38, 41, 44-45, 52, 53, 54, 69, 70, 97, 100, 114, 119-120

Dare, Malkin, on school closures 94, 96, 120

declining enrolments 2, 18, 20, 33, 56, 84, 94, 96

Deloitte, and school reviews 84

Deloitte, and *The Future of Productivity* agenda 11, 120

Delorey, Denise viii, 69, 70, 73-74, 86-87, 100, 114, 120

Delorey, Randy vii, 24, 69, 70, 71, 72, 73-74, 100, 114

Delorey et al. v. SRSB (2012) 19, 73-74, 86-87. 124

Department of Education (Nova Scotia) 2, 3, 4, 17, 20-21 22, 38, 52, 60, 61, 65, 77, 88, 94, 96, 109

Dexter, Premier Darrell 5, 9, 10, 11, 48, 51, 68, 76, 88, 124

Digby Neck, NS 41, 44-45

Dow, Vanda, President of NSHSA 70

Ecology Action Centre 31, 120

Education on a Human Scale (2006) 6, 21, 27, 28, 30, 97, 119

Egan, Sir John, and 2004 UK report 51,

120

Elections Nova Scotia, polls in schools 94

Elliott, Joy, and 2005 CCN report 51, 120

Elliott, Patricia, and Real Renewal, Regina viii, 96, 120

"Evergreening," of rural Nova Scotia 40

Fitch, Sheree 85, 115

Forest Heights Community School (SSRSB) 87

Foster, Mike, and Canmac Economics 8, 10-12, 118

Francis, Debbie viii, 59, 114

Gates Foundation, Bill and Melinda, on small schools 23

Gill, Christopher viii, 70, 72, 84, 94, 115, 120

Gold River-Western Shore School (SSRSB) 87, 115

"grade reconfiguration" agenda 20-21, 57, 59, 87, 121

Greater Halifax Partnership, and "Halifax Hub" plan 11, 120

Greencorn, Troy 52, 53, 121

Guericke, Dan, of Mid-Central Education Cooperative, SD 50

Gunn, Dr. Jim and consulting activities 20 -21, 57, 84, 121

Haight, Larry Donald viii, 61, 71, 72, 92 -93, 94, 100, 114, 121

Halifax Public Libraries, public consultation model 64

Hamm, Premier Dr. John 18

Hebbville and Hebbville Academy (SSRSB) 87, 88

Helmer, Leif vii, 29, 30, 52, 63, 70, 84, 85, 87-88, 96, 100, 114.

"hidden agenda," of AVRSB 57

Howes, Bob, *Chronicle Herald* editor 16

Innovation Lab Schools, in South Dakota 49-50

Ivany, Ray 7, 9

"Jobs Start Here" agenda, and shipbuilding contract 9, 10, 11, 124

Jarvis, Alastair viii, 71, 100

Jennex, Ramona 3, 4, 5, 23, 56, 66-67, 68, 71, 72, 79, 87, 116-117, 121

Johnson, David, of CBU 16

Kids and Learning First (2012) 2, 28, 38, 42, 55, 116, 122

Labor, Sandra vii, 4, 46-47, 70, 100, 114, 121

Laursen, Jens viii, 21, 22, 71, 86, 100, 115, 121

Last Stand, The, and its core message vii, 3, 7

Learning to Leave (2007) 41, 44-45, 54, 119

Leger, Dan 1, 76, 122

Lenihan, Don, of Public Policy Forum 60, 61, 122

Levac, John viii, 95, 115

Lewis, Jamie 93, 94

Lunenburg County, *Vital Signs* report (2010) 44-45, 122

Lunenburg County, school closures and impact 3, 22, 46, 70, 77

Lyson, Dr. Thomas, on loss of small schools 32, 40, 75, 80-81, 83, 122

MacDonald, Mary Jess 33, 34, 73, 122

Mackinnon, Bruce, and school review process cartoon 88

Maitland District School, and hub plan 84-85

McLeod, Cecil viii, 86, 114

McNeil, Stephen, on school reviews 56

McNiven, Dr. Jim, and demographic trends 15-16, 122

Merry, Tim, on public engagement 64, 65

Middle River School, Victoria County, CB 23, 65, 66, 70-71, 100, 109

moratorium, on school closures 2, 4, 5, 18, 19-20, 21-22, 34, 35, 60, 67, 68, 86, 95, 97, 99, 112

Mill Village, and Mill Village Consolidated School (SSRSB) 75,87, 115

Mills, Don (see also "townsizing") 6, 8, 9

Moores, Rev. Vivian, of Riverport, NS 87

Muir, Jamie, and School Reviews 18, 19, 34

Mulcahy, Dennis 6, 21, 27, 28, 30, 38, 97, 119

Murray, Justice Patrick J. 73, 124

networked school communities 49-50

"New Model Schooling," *Chronicle Herald* editorials 6, 66, 119

Newport Station School, and closure battle 23, 57, 58, 59, 65, 76

Nova Scotia School Boards Association (NSSBA) 86, 95

Nova Scotia Small Schools Initiative (NSSSI) vii, 2, 3, 6-7, 56, 66, 68, 72, 76, 94, 112, 114-115.

Nova Scotia Telehealth Network 108

NSSSI on Facebook 72

O'Brien, Dr. Catherine, of CBU 26, 31, 123

Office of the Premier, and Community Relations 5, 67

Oland, Kate vii, 24, 25, 26, 52, 66, 67, 68, 70-71, 72, 100, 106-111, 114

Olivella, Barry viii, 67, 70, 100, 115

Parent Focus Group, on School Reviews (2009-2011) 22-23, 86, 121, 122

Paris, Percy, and rural economic development 16

Pathway to Rural Regeneration (NSSSI Brief, 2013) 7, 75, 112-113, 118

Pentz Elementary School (SSRSB) 70, 87

Petite Plus Hub Plan 77, 84, 87, 119

Petite Riviere Elementary School (SSRSB) 29, 70, 71, 84, 87

Pilkey, Dennis 8, 13-15, 39, 40, 43, 123

Pinch-Worthylake, Nancy (SSRSB Superintendent) 70

place-based curriculum, philosophy and practice 52, 53-54

Pollett, Graham L, MD, 30-31

Prince Edward Island, and rural strategy 37-38

public engagement model (Public Policy Forum, 2012) 60-65

Putnam, Robert, and small schools 18

Quinlan, Kevin, and NSCC Truro 84, 114

Rafuse, Trish, of Cambridge, NS 58

Rees, Maurice, and *Shoreline Journal* 17, 114

Regional Development Authorities (RDAs) 10, 36, 53

Rev. H.J. Macdonald School, Heatherton, NS 19, 25, 34, 69, 72-73, 120

Reversing the Tide (BC, 2009) 39, 120

Rhude, Steven vii, viii, 52, 59, 70, 100, 114

River John Consolidated School, and Hub Plan 85

Riverport Consolidated School, and Save Riverport Campaign 3, 71, 77, 86

rural decline, and depopulation 1-2 , 8, 10, 11-12, 13, 38, 122

rural development strategy, for NS 36, 38-40, 42, 46,47, 60 -61, 67, 98-99, 113, 121

rural education 2, 6, 19, 75, 81, 119

rural education, in NS 2, 4, 36, 37, 40, 44-45, 46-47, 55, 71, 90

rural population, of Nova Scotia 1, 8, 36-37, 75

rural school busing (see school bus rides)

Rural Schools Online Education Network (NL) 4

rural strategies, in Canada 36-38, 49, 100

Samson, Jamie 73

Save Community Schools (Heatherton, NS) vii, 69, 70, 71, 100, 114

school bus rides, and problems of 17, 19, 23, 26-27, 30-31, 67, 88, 107, 109-110

school consolidation, philosophy and impact 2, 6, 17, 18, 20, 27, 30, 32, 46, 53-54, 55, 59, 81, 96, 120, 124

Schools at the Centre (NSSSD Brief, 2012) 3-5, 6, 35, 46, 66, 67, 68, 72, 88, 95, 98-100, 123

school review process, in NS 5, 18-20, 21-22, 33, 53, 56, 58, 69, 70, 73, 75, 76, 83, 85, 96, 101-105, 116-117

school review process, criticisms of 5, 7,

18-20, 21-23, 24-26, 33-35, 55, 56, 60-65, 66-67, 71, 86-87, 89, 92, 97, 98-99, 112-113, 116, 121
School Study Committees, role and impact 22, 24-25
Schools Plus, and community schools 38, 79, 80, 94-95, 109, 116, 118
Schopp, Melody (Education Secretary, SD) 49-50
Shatford Memorial Elementary School, Hubbards, NS vii, 46-47, 70-71, 121
Sher, Jonathan P., on rural schools 6
Small Isolated Schools, and grants 24, 38, 50, 110, 116
Small School Summit vii, 7, 33, 46, 70.
Smaller, Saner Successful Schools (2002) 49
Sobel, David 52
social capital, and rebuilding of 7, 30, 75, 80
social prosperity framework, in Nova Scotia 48, 50-51, 123
social sustainability, philosophy and principles 4, 6, 51, 97, 120
Social Sustainability Framework (Young Foundation, 2011) 75, 81- 83, 113, 125
South Shore Regional School Board (SSRSB) and school closures 3, 22, 45, 69-70, 75, 82, 87-88
Stevens, Jamie, of New Glasgow, NS 86
St.Mary's Bay Academy, proposed 2012 expansion 91-92
Stockton, Ron vii, 67, 70, 100, 101- 105, 115
Strongest Families Institute 108
Successful Schools for Successful Students (AVRSB) 56, 57-59, 62-63, 67, 118
Sullivan-Corney, Judith , and one-person SSRSB 70
"Sunday Drive Hangover," and mentality (Kate Oland, 2012) 106, 107
Surette, Ralph 11, 124
Sustainable Communities initiative (NS, 1999) 48

Tate, Margo (AVRSB Superintendent) 57, 58, 59
Taylor, Abby viii, 85, 115
Theriault, Harold (Junior) MLA 41, 91

Thompson, Ian, of *Chronicle Herald* 16
Thompson, Trudy (chair, CCRSB) 85
Three Mile Plains School (AVRSB) 58, 59
Tidd, Donna (chair, TCRSB) 92
Tim Horton's Bridgewater, coffee chat 85
Toney, Gerald (Mi'kmaw elder) 55, 58
"townsizing" 6, 8-9
Tri-County Regional School Board (TCRSB) 34, 72, 75, 91, 93, 94, 95, 124
two Nova Scotias, and "the other Nova Scotia" 1-2

Union of Nova Scotia Municipalities (UNSM) 8, 11-12, 76, 118

Vanishing Schools, Threatened Communities (2011) viii, 18, 24, 118
Virtual School, virtual schooling in Nova Scotia 4, 6, 42, 66, 68, 99, 109, 113

Wamboldt, Michelle vii, 20, 24, 67, 70, 100, 114.
Weaving the Threads (NS 2010) 42, 50, 123
Wentworth Consolidated School 19, 75, 86
West Richmond Education Centre, Evanston, NS 34, 100, 114
Weymouth Consolidated School, and Save Weymouth School Campaign 28, 61, 72, 90 – 94
Wallin, Dawn C., and rural education survey (2009) 48-49, 124
Willick, Frances, *Chronicle Herald* Education reporter viii, 5, 86-87, 88, 89, 94, 125
Windsor Forks District School (AVRSB) 58, 59, 121

Yarmouth ferry, cancellation of 10
Yuill, Cathrine, of Maitland, NS viii, 84-85, 86, 114